the
essential
kitchen

Christine McFadden

foreword by Charlie Trotter
photography by Mark Williams

the
essential
kitchen

Basic Tools, Recipes, and Tips
for a Complete Kitchen

RIZZOLI
NEW YORK

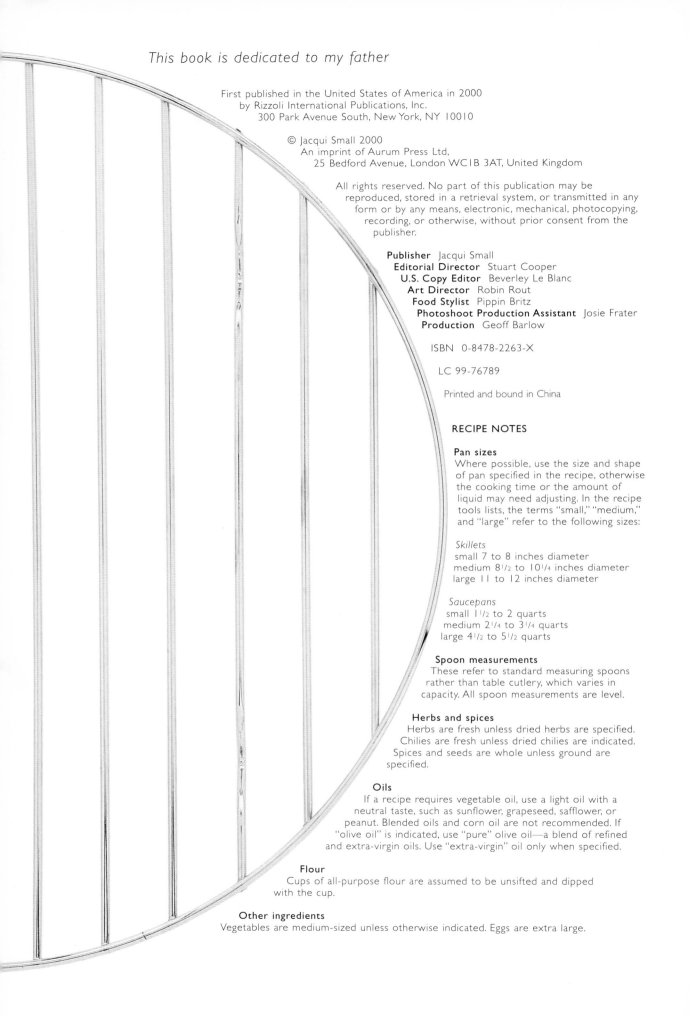

This book is dedicated to my father

First published in the United States of America in 2000
by Rizzoli International Publications, Inc.
300 Park Avenue South, New York, NY 10010

© Jacqui Small 2000
An imprint of Aurum Press Ltd,
25 Bedford Avenue, London WC1B 3AT, United Kingdom

Publisher Jacqui Small
Editorial Director Stuart Cooper
U.S. Copy Editor Beverley Le Blanc
Art Director Robin Rout
Food Stylist Pippin Britz
Photoshoot Production Assistant Josie Frater
Production Geoff Barlow

ISBN 0-8478-2263-X

LC 99-76789

Printed and bound in China

RECIPE NOTES

Pan sizes

Where possible, use the size and shape
of pan specified in the recipe, otherwise
the cooking time or the amount of
liquid may need adjusting. In the recipe
tools lists, the terms "small," "medium,"
and "large" refer to the following sizes:

Skillets
small 7 to 8 inches diameter
medium 8 1/2 to 10 1/4 inches diameter
large 11 to 12 inches diameter

Saucepans
small 1 1/2 to 2 quarts
medium 2 1/4 to 3 1/4 quarts
large 4 1/2 to 5 1/2 quarts

Spoon measurements

These refer to standard measuring spoons
rather than table cutlery, which varies in
capacity. All spoon measurements are level.

Herbs and spices

Herbs are fresh unless dried herbs are specified.
Chilies are fresh unless dried chilies are indicated.
Spices and seeds are whole unless ground are
specified.

Oils

If a recipe requires vegetable oil, use a light oil with a
neutral taste, such as sunflower, grapeseed, safflower, or
peanut. Blended oils and corn oil are not recommended. If
"olive oil" is indicated, use "pure" olive oil—a blend of refined
and extra-virgin oils. Use "extra-virgin" oil only when specified.

Flour

Cups of all-purpose flour are assumed to be unsifted and dipped
with the cup.

Other ingredients

Vegetables are medium-sized unless otherwise indicated. Eggs are extra large.

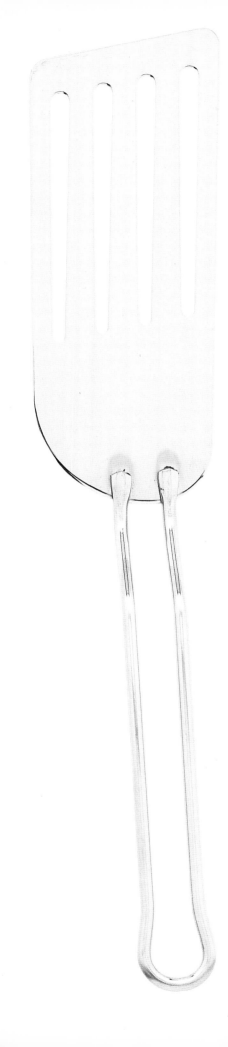

contents

foreword

Chefs and home cooks alike will agree that raw ingredients are a thing of beauty—but so too are the tools. A well-crafted tool becomes an extension of the body, turning the raw ingredients into the beautiful dishes we love.

At my restaurant, I find great joy in gazing about the kitchen and seeing the chefs use a myriad of different implements to prepare food for our guests. Some of the items we use are modern, time-saving tools, such as food processors and electric juicers, but many others—knives, mandolines, mortar and pestle, copper pans and bowls, for instance—are the same tried-and-true varieties that have been used for hundreds of years.

There is no substitute for well-crafted tools. Although they may cost more initially, they can last a lifetime. In fact, I still use my grandmother's old potato ricer. Though it has a few little dents, it works perfectly, and each time I take it out I am reminded of Sunday dinners at her house.

Knowing which tools to choose can be difficult, but *The Essential Kitchen* will help guide you through the process. With photos and descriptions of over 400 cooking tools, along with clear instructions on their use, it is an essential volume for every cook.

Charlie Trotter

introduction

There was a time not so very long ago when the home cook had to search for kitchen tools in dusty hardware stores or make do with the limited selection offered by department stores. If you were more enterprising, you could venture into one of those awe-inspiring but impersonal shops that supply chefs and caterers. Nowadays, the choice of kitchen tools and cookware has proliferated beyond belief. Along with cookbooks and TV cookery shows, there is an abundance of kitchen stores, specialized mail-order companies, and websites, from which an astonishing range of kitchenware can be purchased. Along with quantity, quality has improved too. Knives, pots, and pans come in sleek designs and state-of-the-art materials.

While there is no shortage of options, there is a lack of accessible information on how and what to choose. For example, how do you find

As well as detailed information on tools and cookware, the book includes mouth-watering recipes that put them to good use—several contributed by well-known chefs and food writers; the rest are my own.

I have not included every tool or piece of equipment, nor are all the items featured necessarily essential. The main criteria for inclusion were efficiency and comfort in use, durability in relation to cost, and, finally, appearance. No matter how design-conscious a tool is, I find that function invariably wins out over style—in other words, if the shape of an item is determined by its use, it tends to be more credible than one that bows to the dictates of fashion. That said, I have included a few "designer" items simply because they hold some personal appeal. You will also find a few ugly ducklings included for the same reason.

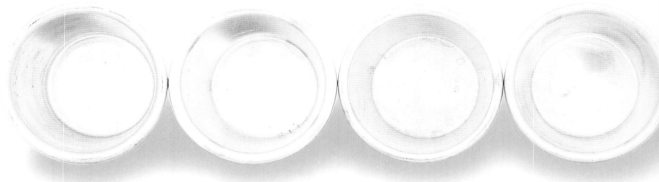

out which type of knife should be used for a particular job? Should the blade be straight or curved, rigid or flexible, long or short? Why do some skillets have lids? Why do some pans have long handles and others short? Is stainless steel better than cast iron?

This book answers all these questions and many more. It provides essential information for evaluating and choosing new tools and cookware—whether it's a humble potato peeler or an expensive electric stand mixer. You'll find explanations of how tools work, and how to use them in the most efficient way. There is also a guide to the pros and cons of different materials and how to care for them. With this sort of information under your belt, you can make informed choices when you purchase equipment, and you will be able to cook with greater confidence and efficiency.

What you have in your kitchen is very much a personal choice, depending on how you live and what you like to cook. Build your "batterie de cuisine" gradually, allowing it to evolve as your cooking style develops. I tend to use the same trusty old tools and pots and pans for years, but when my cooking changes in some way—perhaps as a result of foreign travel, or reading something inspiring, or discovering a new ingredient—I indulge in a new piece of equipment, and what a pleasure that is. It is always a joy to find a tool that makes preparation easier, or a pan that cooks more efficiently, or one that is simply so pleasing that you never want to put it away.

Whether you are a novice or a proficient cook, I hope this book will inspire and inform, as well as open up the path to new and exciting culinary experiences.

material choice

This list explains briefly the pros and cons of the principal materials from which cooking equipment is made, and provides guidance on care and cleaning.

ALUMINUM

Uses Pots, pans, bakeware, roasting pans, kettles, wrapping foil.
Pros Inexpensive, lightweight, conducts heat well and evenly as long as the gauge is heavy enough.
Cons Reacts with substances in food and therefore will discolor certain foods or impart a metallic taste. The metal itself tends to discolor and pit. Thin-gauge aluminum warps easily and heats unevenly.
Care Wash with hot soapy water, using a scouring pad if necessary. Remove stains by boiling in a weak solution of vinegar or cream of tartar.

ANODIZED ALUMINUM

Uses As for aluminum.
Pros Anodizing is an electrochemical process that gives aluminum a hard, dense oxide coating that resists corrosion. Hard-anodizing does not just produce a coating—it changes the molecular structure of aluminum, making it harder than steel while maintaining excellent heat distribution.
Cons Dishwasher detergents cause colored anodized aluminum pans to fade.
Care Wash with hot, soapy water. Do not use scouring pads.

CAST IRON

Uses Pots, pans, griddles, grill pans, Dutch ovens, baking dishes.
Pros Durable, strong, does not warp, conducts heat evenly and retains it well. Marvelous for long, slow cooking.
Cons Very heavy, so best for a pan that remains fairly static during cooking—e.g. a casserole. Its density makes it slow to heat. If dropped on a hard floor, it may break. If uncoated (with enamel or a nonstick surface), it needs seasoning with oil to prevent sticking and rusting.
Care Avoid washing uncoated cast iron; wipe with paper towels. Remove stuck-on food by lightly scouring under hot running water. Dry well and coat with oil before storing. Brush the cooking surface with oil before each use, then wipe off before adding oil for cooking. Wash coated cast iron with hot, soapy water but do not scour. To remove stubborn residue, leave the pan to soak for an hour or two.

COPPER

Uses Pots, pans, gratin dishes, roasting pans, egg bowls, molds.
Pros The traditional choice of chefs as it is unbeaten for rapid and uniform heat conduction. Lasts forever.
Cons Expensive and needs cosseting. If unlined, reacts with most foods, causing discoloration and mild toxicity if contact is prolonged. Unlined copper does not retain heat well. The traditional tin lining blisters or melts if overheated. Silver lining blackens on contact with the air and sulfurous compounds in some foods. Needs re-lining periodically.
Care Wash with hot, soapy water. Never use scouring pads. Soak to remove stuck-on food. Dry with soft cloth to bring up the shine. Use a proprietary cleaner for the outside, or rub with salt and vinegar or salt and lemon juice. Buff up the inside of silver-lined pans with a silver cleaner.

EARTHENWARE

Uses Casseroles, mixing bowls, gratin dishes, baking stones.
Pros Nonreactive, inexpensive, retains heat well and, as it is porous, moisture. Excellent for slow, moist cooking in the oven, or for use in a microwave oven.
Cons Dislikes sudden or extreme temperature changes. Not flameproof, but good-quality earthenware can be used on a heat diffuser over a low flame. Large rectangular and oval oven dishes are more prone to heat fracture than round ones.
Care Wash glazed, or partially glazed, pots with hot, soapy water without scouring. Completely unglazed pots such as a potato baker should be scrubbed clean with salty water. Don't use detergent as this will taint the food.

POLYTETRAFLUOROETHYLENE (nonstick coatings)

Trade names include Probon, Silverstone, Tefal, Teflon, Xylan.
Uses Pots, pans, roasting pans, grill pans, griddles, casseroles, bakeware, utensils.
Pros Modern nonstick coatings are tough and long-lasting.

Nonreactive and easy to clean, they are a boon for pans used for foods that stick, such as milk, and vital for low-fat cooking.
Cons The coating eventually wears off. Use utensils made of materials that are softer than the coating to prolong its life (e.g. wood, rubber, or plastic). Not usually dishwasher-proof.
Care According to directions. Avoid scouring and abrasive powders. Soak in warm water to remove stuck-on food.

PORCELAIN

Uses Soufflé dishes, ramekins, gratin dishes, tart pans.
Pros Looks fragile but can withstand heat so makes excellent oven-to-tableware. Retains heat and conducts it evenly. Can be used briefly under the broiler. Nonporous and nonreactive.
Cons Extreme temperature changes cause cracking. Needs a heat-diffuser if used on the stovetop. Can be hard to clean.
Care Wash in hot, soapy water. Soak to remove stuck-on food. If scouring is needed, use a nylon scouring pad.

STAINLESS STEEL

Uses Pots, pans, roasting pans and racks, bowls, kettles, knives, utensils.
Pros Long-lasting and hygienic. Contains chrome, which is what makes it stainless, rustproof, and nonreactive. Stainless-steel pots and pans also contain nickel. They may be described as 18/10, which means the ratio of chrome to nickel is !8% and 10% respectively. It is virtually immune to corrosion or pitting. Stainless steel used for most kitchen knives contains a lower level of chrome—at least 12%—and 0.15–0.80% carbon. Because of the reduction in chrome, it is more prone to staining, but the carbon provides strength.
Cons Poor and uneven conductor of heat. Manufacturers overcome this by giving pans a three- or five-layer sandwich base containing highly conductive metals such as aluminum or copper. Good stainless-steel pans have a base containing at least $3/16$ inch of aluminum or $1/8$ inch of copper. In the best-quality pans, the sandwiched layer continues up the sides, which prevents hot food from sizzling and sticking.

Stainless steel is not entirely stainless—it will discolor, stain, or spot if left in contact with hard water, salt water, lemon, vinegar, or even some detergents if not rinsed and dried carefully after washing. Small pits may form.
Care Clean with hot, soapy water, using a nylon scourer if necessary. Avoid bleach or harsh abrasives. Soak burnt-on foods. Remove stubborn stains with a stainless-steel cleaner.

STONEWARE

Uses Casseroles, storage jars, bowls.
Pros Stronger than earthenware as it's fired at a higher temperature. Nonporous so does not need glazing. Ideal for dishes that need long, slow cooking in the oven.
Cons Does not take kindly to radical temperature changes.
Care As for glazed earthenware.

TEMPERED GLASS

Flameproof glass (Pyroflam), and ovenproof glass (Duralex, Pyrex)
Uses Flameproof: saucepans, casseroles, baking dishes. Ovenproof: Dutch ovens, gratin dishes, bowls, measuring jugs.
Pros Both types retain heat well, are nonreactive and are ideal for the microwave. Flameproof glass can be used on the stovetop and in the oven.
Cons Flameproof glass is expensive. It conducts heat unevenly, so develops hot spots on the stovetop, causing food to stick. Ovenproof glass may crack at extreme temperature changes. It must be used with a diffuser on the stovetop.
Care Soak in hot soapy water to remove burnt-on food. Avoid metal scourers or harsh abrasives.

TITANIUM

Uses Dutch ovens, skillets, sauté pans, grill pans.
Pros A rock-hard, lightweight metal that is naturally nonstick and virtually corrosion-resistant. It is great for low-fat cooking—the food sizzles round the pan with no oil. You can use metal utensils without causing damage.
Cons Expensive. Cannot be used on induction stovetops.
Care Wash with warm, soapy water; do not scour.

VITREOUS ENAMEL

Uses Pots, pans, Dutch ovens, pie dishes, bowls, roasting pans.
Pros Used to coat cast iron, aluminum, or steel. Gives an easy-to-clean, nonporous coating that is taint- and scratch-proof.
Cons May chip if used with sharp-edged metal utensils.
Care Wash with hot, soapy water. Do not scrub with harsh abrasives. Leave to soak if necessary.

cutting
peeling
and
piercing

basic blades

Next to your hands, the knife is probably the most important tool in the kitchen. If you buy good knives, use them with care and respect, and keep them in good condition, they should last your entire cooking life.

All knife blades are made of steel, which is why, traditionally, they have been manufactured in metal-working towns. The composition of steel varies, the amount of carbon present determining the blade's ability to hold its edge. Traditional carbon-steel blades are sharper, but the metal stains and corrodes, so other agents must be added. "Stainless" steel contains chromium, which is rustproof but also more difficult to sharpen. Today, good-quality knives are made of high-carbon, no-stain steel, which is not quite stainless. Despite the carbon element, these knives neither rust nor corrode.

Blades are either forged or stamped, and the difference in quality is obvious. Forged blades are evenly balanced and beautifully tapered at the cutting edge, which results in greater flexibility. A stamped-bladed knife is thin and flat, and feels handle-heavy. You'll need to grip it more tightly and exert more pressure toward the front to compensate.

1 Bread knife The long, serrated blade cuts through bread or any other soft food with a tough crust or skin. Don't use serrated blades for cutting meat or dense-fleshed fruit and vegetables—you'll end up with a jagged mess.

2 Cook's knife The undisputed workhorse of the kitchen, the cook's knife has a characteristically wide blade and a graceful curve along the entire length of the cutting edge—designed to cope with repeated impact against a chopping board. Use it for chopping or dicing anything from hefty lumps of meat to the finest of herbs. Cook's knives come in a variety of lengths; an 8- to 10-inch blade is the most useful for the home.

3 Utility knife As its name suggests, this knife can be used for a variety of cutting jobs, including slicing, peeling, paring, and, depending on the length of the blade, carving. Although it is not designed for impact (the blade is narrower and less curved than the cook's knife), it can cope with chopping small amounts of not-too-tough food such as mushrooms or shrimp. Look for a knife with a 5- to 7-inch blade.

4 Tomato/sandwich knife Invaluable for tasks for which a bread knife would be too big. The serrated edge is useful for slicing food with a tough exterior and a soft center, such as salami.

5 Paring knife Basically a miniature version of the cook's knife, a paring knife is used for peeling, scraping, and slicing small fruits and vegetables. It is perhaps easier to use than a cook's knife when finely chopping garlic and ginger. The blade must be short, about 3 to 4 inches.

6 Vegetable knife With its slightly upturned tip and short, curved blade, this knife is handy for peeling small, round vegetables and for gouging eyes from potatoes.

7 Knife block Instead of the usual slots, which can be awkward to use, this block has nylon filaments that hold the knives in place without scratching them.

Choosing knives

Choose knives individually—don't be tempted to buy sets. Hold a knife to assess it. It should feel heavy for its size and evenly weighted, neither front- nor back-heavy. Do not be put off by weight—a heavy knife is more effective than a light one and requires less effort to use.

The handle of the knife should be comfortable to hold. If it has rivets, the tops should be smooth and flush. Make sure the bolster (see "Knife speak," page 12) fuses smoothly with the handle.

Each knife is designed for a specific purpose, so think about the types of food you regularly prepare before making a choice. Ideally, you should try to use the correct knife for the job. If funds are short, though, opt for the best quality and have fewer knives. It is possible to manage with one decent cook's knife and a paring knife. However, the six basic knives shown will give you more scope.

Knife care

Store your knives in a knife block so the blades are protected and the knives are easily accessible. A wall-mounted magnetic rack is another option, though some people question the safety of these (see "Knife safety," page 12). Don't store knives loose in a drawer, as the cutting edges can be damaged by impact with other knives and utensils.

Damage will be caused, too, by dumping knives in the sink. Some of the better-quality knives are dishwasher-proof, but if yours are not, wash, rinse, and dry them individually immediately after use. Don't leave knives to soak.

To keep your knives in prime condition, give each one a few strokes on a steel whenever you use it. Fast, flamboyant sharpening is not essential. More important is maintaining a 20° angle and sharpening the full length of the blade (see "Using a steel," above).

Treat the blade with care by using a wooden or polyethylene board to chop on. Don't use a plate or the countertop, as hard materials such as glass, granite, or metal will harm the cutting edge.

Using a steel: method 1 Hold the steel vertically on a firm surface. Grasp the knife low on the handle, with the blade at a 20° angle to the steel. Bring the knife down and across the steel, drawing it to you so the tip meets the steel at the base. Reverse the action, holding the other side of the blade against the other side of the steel and pushing away from you. Repeat both actions until the blade is sharp.

Using a steel: method 2 Grasp the steel in one hand and the knife in the other. Place the handle ends of each together, with the blade at a 20° angle to the steel. Raise your elbows and part your hands so the blade travels up the steel, finishing with the tip of the blade against the steel. Repeat, holding the other side of the blade against the other side of the steel. Repeat both movements until the blade is sharp.

8 V-shaped sharpener The outer casing houses cunningly arranged, crossed pairs of steel rods set on springs and positioned at the 20° sharpening angle. The rods mimic the action of a conventional steel as the blade is drawn across them. This is a good tool for those who have difficulty using a steel.

9 Carborundum stone Carborundum is the trade name for a group of rock-hard abrasives, usually composed of silicon carbide. The stones are useful for smoothing out small scratches or indentations. The best ones have two grades of surface: fairly fine on one side and coarser on the other. Most stones are rectangular in shape, though the one shown here resembles a short steel. To use a stone, first lubricate it with water or cooking oil. Holding the knife blade at a 15 to 20° angle to the stone, pass the length of the blade over the stone. Turn the knife over and repeat in the opposite direction. Repeat both movements several times until the blade is sharp.

10 Sharpening steel Somewhat surprisingly, a steel works not by sharpening, but by realigning the molecules that form the cutting edge. They are knocked out of alignment by repeated chopping.

A steel needs to be made of a substance that is harder than the tool to be sharpened. Ceramic or diamond-coated steels are hardest of all. Traditional steels are cylindrical with grooves running along the length of the rod, but some are oval or flat and others have smoother surfaces. The finer the surface, the sharper will be the finish. Choose a steel with a shaft that is longer than the blade of your biggest knife.

This superb steel is diamond-coated and has a flat, relatively smooth surface, providing greater contact than a cylindrical steel.

8

9 **10**

beyond basics

As you become more experienced, you will undoubtedly want to add to your knife collection. The knives shown here are for specialized tasks or for dealing with specific foods. Some of them are expensive, but good knives are good to have, and once you've got them you can easily justify their existence. Buy oysters, eat grapefruit, or fillet your own fish....

Knife speak

O **Butt** The downward-curving tip of the handle. This cushions your hand against the impact of chopping.

O **Handle** The part attached to the tang. Make sure it feels comfortable and is neither too large nor too small for you to grip firmly.

O **Tang** The unsharpened part of the knife blade that extends into the handle. The longer the tang, the better balanced the knife will be.

O **Bolster** The splayed metal section on a forged blade that butts up against the handle. The bolster strengthens the blade and keeps your hand away from the cutting area.

O **Blade** The flat part of the knife that forms the cutting edge.

Knife safety
Knives are dangerous tools. That said, if they are treated with respect rather than with presumption, they will be less likely to cause accidents.

O *Never* test for sharpness by running your finger along the cutting edge. If you cannot resist touching the blade, brush your finger lightly *across* it.

O A sharp knife is safer than a blunt one. A blunt knife needs more pressure to cut and could slip.

O If you use a magnetic rack for storage, make sure it is out of reach of children and pets.

O Don't leave knives hidden under soapy water in the sink.

O Don't use a knife with a greasy handle.

O If you leave a knife on the countertop, ensure that neither the handle nor blade protrude over the edge. The knife can easily be grabbed by a child or knocked onto the floor or, worse still, onto someone's foot.

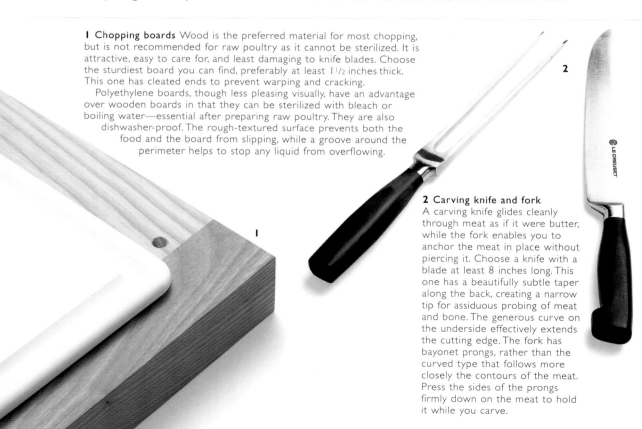

1 Chopping boards Wood is the preferred material for most chopping, but is not recommended for raw poultry as it cannot be sterilized. It is attractive, easy to care for, and least damaging to knife blades. Choose the sturdiest board you can find, preferably at least 1 1/2 inches thick. This one has cleated ends to prevent warping and cracking.

Polyethylene boards, though less pleasing visually, have an advantage over wooden boards in that they can be sterilized with bleach or boiling water—essential after preparing raw poultry. They are also dishwasher-proof. The rough-textured surface prevents both the food and the board from slipping, while a groove around the perimeter helps to stop any liquid from overflowing.

2 Carving knife and fork
A carving knife glides cleanly through meat as if it were butter, while the fork enables you to anchor the meat in place without piercing it. Choose a knife with a blade at least 8 inches long. This one has a beautifully subtle taper along the back, creating a narrow tip for assiduous probing of meat and bone. The generous curve on the underside effectively extends the cutting edge. The fork has bayonet prongs, rather than the curved type that follows more closely the contours of the meat. Press the sides of the prongs firmly down on the meat to hold it while you carve.

3 Ham/smoked salmon slicer This is used for carving thin, elongated slices. The blade is narrow and reasonably flexible, and must be at least 10 inches long. It has a very slight taper through its thickness, enabling you to produce straight slices, rather than veering diagonally off-course—an effect caused by a more pronounced taper.

4 Freezer knife A freezer knife is not wholeheartedly recommended, as food texture and appearance may suffer if you hack at it while still frozen—it is better to let food defrost before cutting. If you do buy one, a strong, deeply toothed blade is a must. The blade should be longer than the largest item you are likely to cut.

5 Filleting knife This elegant knife has a thin, gently curved blade, which is sufficiently pliable to remain in close contact with the contours of fish or poultry. The blade needs to be at least 7 inches long, and should be kept scrupulously sharp in order to do its job.

6 Boning knife A boning knife has a tapered blade with a sharp point. Blades are flexible or rigid, and 5/8 to 1 inch in width. A wide, rigid blade is good for large cuts of meat with simple bones, while a narrow, flexible blade copes with poultry or fish.

7 "Universal" cheese knife The blade of this knife has holes that prevent cheese from sticking to it, while the serrated cutting edge copes with hard cheese. The forked tip assists with transferring cheese to a plate.

8 Parmesan knife The rigid, leaf-shaped blade of this knife extracts chunks from hard cheeses such as Parmesan. Embed it in the cheese and twist.

9 Grapefruit knife The long, thin, serrated blade, with a curved tip, neatly cuts between the pith and flesh, following the contours of the fruit.

10 Oyster knife Two short, arrow-shaped cutting edges prize open the shell, breaking its vacuum. The guard at the hilt protects the hand and also prevents the knife from thrusting into the shell and out the other side. The pointed tip is used to sever the oyster meat from the shell.

11 Cleaver Equally useful for demolishing bones or shredding scallions, the blade of the cleaver is thick and rigid throughout most of its width, before tapering abruptly to a sharp bevel. The greater the weight, the less effort required, so buy the heaviest cleaver you can use with comfort. A 6-inch blade is about the right length. This modern-style cleaver has a seamless blade and handle, which makes it easy to clean. Use the hole to hang your cleaver on the wall out of harm's way.

Japanese knives

12 Sometimes called a sashimi knife, the long yanagi is single-beveled like the deba (see below). The blade glides through raw fish, producing immaculately straight, paper-thin slices for sushi. The knife is also used to slice and chop vegetables, and to produce intricate Oriental garnishes.

13 Somewhat surprisingly, the medium-length, wide-bladed deba is used for the delicate task of boning and filleting fish. This is made possible by Japanese-style grinding, in which the blade is beveled over a wide area on one side and the opposite side is left flat. This creates a razor-sharp, acutely angled cutting edge that slips effortlessly between flesh and bone.

Filleting flat fish

1 Place the fish on a chopping board. With the point of a filleting knife, cut the fish to the bone behind the gills, across the tail, and around the edge of the flesh. This defines the shape of the fillets. Slice along the backbone from head to tail, down to the bone.

2 Holding the knife almost flat, slide it under the flesh, beginning at the backbone. Keeping the knife flat, use a gentle sawing motion to ease away the first fillet from the bones. Repeat on the other side of the backbone for the second fillet.

3 Turn the fish over. Use the knife point to define the shape of the third and fourth fillets, and cut down the backbone as described in step 1. Ease the fillets gently away from the bones as described in step 2.

Boning a whole chicken breast

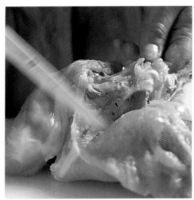

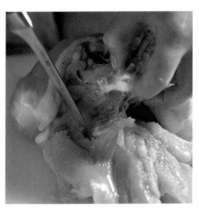

1 Place skin-side down on a polyethylene chopping board. Grip the breast at each end and twist backward to separate the breast- and collarbones. Poke your fingers into the flesh to locate the wishbone and remove it with the tip of a boning knife.

2 With the skin-side facing down, use a gentle scraping motion with the tip end of the knife blade to carefully cut away the flesh from each side of the breastbone. Once the flesh is cut free, remove the breastbone.

3 Cut the flesh away from the ribs, following the contours of the bones and cutting as close to them as possible. Remove the ribs and cut out the remaining cartilage. Trim the breasts neatly according to your chosen recipe.

Carving a leg of lamb

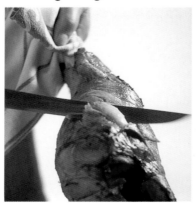

1 Place the meat on a carving board with the meatier side uppermost. Wrap the shank end in a napkin. Carve thin slices from the rounded side of the leg, cutting away from you and almost parallel with the bone.

2 Turn the leg over and carve about the same number of slices from the opposite side, slicing along the length of the leg and almost parallel with the bone.

3 Insert the carving knife at the shank end of the leg and carve small, thin slices of meat from the bone. Try to carve an equal number of slices from each part of the leg.

Hong Kong-style broccoli and baby corn

Contributed by Ken Hom, a leading authority on Asian cooking, this easy-to-prepare stir-fry puts the cleaver to good use. As Ken says, "Once you gain facility with a cleaver, you will see how it can be used on all types of food to slice, dice, chop, fillet, shred, crush, or whatever."

Serves 4 to 6 as a side dish or light meal

Tools	Ingredients
preparation bowls	1 ³/₄ oz. Chinese dried black mushrooms
strainer	1 lb. broccoli
cleaver	¹/₂ lb. baby corn
vegetable peeler	1 tsp. salt
	¹/₂ tsp. freshly ground black pepper
large saucepan	1 tsp. sugar
	1 tbsp. Shaoxing rice wine or pale dry sherry
wok or large skillet	1 tbsp. light soy sauce
wok ladle or long-handled wooden spoon	3 tbsp. oyster sauce or dark soy sauce
	1 ¹/₂ tbsp. peanut oil
	2 tsp. dark sesame oil

1 Soak the black mushrooms in warm water for 20 minutes. Drain them and squeeze out the excess liquid. Remove and discard the stems and finely shred the caps into thin strips. Set aside.

2 Separate the broccoli heads into small flowerets, then peel and slice the stems. Blanch the broccoli pieces and baby corn in a large pot of boiling salted water for 3 minutes, then immerse them in cold water. Drain thoroughly.

3 Combine the salt, pepper, sugar, rice wine, soy sauce, and oyster sauce in a small bowl.

4 Heat a wok or large skillet over high heat. Add the peanut oil and when it is very hot and slightly smoking, add the broccoli, corn, and mushrooms. Stir-fry for 3 minutes.

5 Add the seasoning and sauce mixture and continue stir-frying at a moderate-to-high heat for 2 minutes, until the vegetables are heated through.

6 Add the sesame oil and stir-fry for another 30 seconds. The vegetables are ready to serve.

Using a cleaver Hold the food with your fingertips curled under so your middle knuckles act as a guide for the blade. Don't raise the cleaver higher than your knuckles. Position the blade about ¹/₈ inch from the edge of the food and slice downward. Control the thickness of the slices by moving your fingers either away from or toward the edge being cut. To slice diagonally, position your fingers at a slant and use this to guide the blade.

more cutting tools

These tools are designed to ease difficult or time-consuming food preparation tasks, such as slicing, chopping, shredding, and peeling. The end result is usually neater than it would be if you had not used the tool. These are not mere gadgets; they've all been around for years and have proved their worth.

Vegetable peelers
1 Practical and economical, the all-metal swivel peeler has a central slot that is wide and long enough not to trap peelings. The slot is sharpened on both sides, so it suits both left- and right-handed users. The swivel action enables the tool to follow more accurately the contours of the item being peeled, reducing wastage.
2 Instantly recognizable by its string-wrapped handle, this traditional British peeler has a V-shaped blade with a narrow slot, which can become clogged. The sharpened tip digs out blemishes.
3 This sleek, Y-shaped peeler was originally designed for the manually disabled. It has a swivel blade, and the handle is made of a nonslip rubber and polypropylene composite. The extra thickness makes it easier to grip.

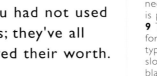

4 Canelle knife or lemon stripper A protruding, V-shaped tooth gouges out thin lengths of peel from citrus fruits. The knife can also be used to cut narrow grooves from unpeeled cucumbers or mushrooms, creating a scalloped edge when the vegetables are sliced. The tool shown is for right-handed use only, though left-handed models are available.

5 Citrus zester Five sharp-edged holes set into an angled blade tip produce flavorsome wisps of citrus zest to use for decorating cakes and desserts. The blade's shallow angle ensures that it cuts only into the zest, or outer surface of the peel, rather than into the bitter pith.

Bean slicers
8 The small plastic slicer works like magic on runner beans, simultaneously removing the strings and slicing the bean into spaghetti-like strands. Simply insert a bean into the hole and push it through the four blades. When it emerges, grasp the end and pull. Beans need to be crisp and firm, and the tool is practical for small amounts only.
9 This sturdy, cast-iron slicer is useful for processing large quantities of any type of bean. Beans are fed through slots into the path of three very sharp blades set into a disc that revolves as you turn the crank handle. They emerge as paper-thin, diagonally cut slices with no evidence of stringiness. One possible drawback is that the clamp cannot be attached to a countertop that is thicker than 1 1/4 inches.

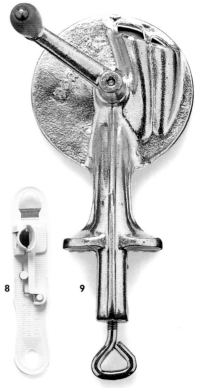

6 Pizza wheel When it comes to dividing up pizza, the pizza wheel outclasses even the sharpest knife. The wobble-free, circular blade carves cleanly through topping and crust, yielding neat, manageable slices. The guard protects your fingers from slipping onto the blade.

7 Cheese plane This efficient tool was originally designed for shaving wafer-thin slices from Scandinavian cheeses too pungent to be eaten in larger amounts. The angled cutting edge guides slices through a slot and onto the spade-shaped blade. The blade supports the cheese and stops it from splitting as it is transported to your plate.

10 Hard-boiled egg slicer Ten taut wires attached to a frame cut cleanly and evenly through white and yolk. Since the wires do not drag, the yolk does not crumble.

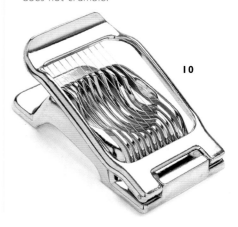

Mandoline

11 The stainless steel and black fiberglass model zips through vegetables with the utmost precision. Depending on the shape and position of the blade, you can quickly cut any firm vegetable into slices, matchsticks, waffles, or ripples. Just hold the piece of vegetable firmly and pass it across the blades. There are alternative blades, and an adjustable gauge determines thickness of cut. Rubber feet hold it safely in place, and a guard protects your fingers. However, it is expensive.

12 Much cheaper, but altogether cruder, is the wooden mandoline. Though it has drawbacks—namely a tendency to warp, and a lack of supporting feet—it is a classic, and, unless you want one hundred percent precision, it does the job perfectly well.

13 Mezzaluna Used mainly for cutting herbs, the mezzaluna ("half-moon" in Italian) works on the same principle as a cook's knife—a curved blade rocks back and forth over the material to be chopped. The two handles enable you to exert an even downward pressure, while the crescent-shaped blade increases the length of the cutting edge. Some types have two or even three blades. Though this speeds up chopping, more time needs to be spent scraping herbs from the blades.

14 Hachoir The half-moon cutting blade and identically shaped bowl are ideal for chopping ginger, garlic, or small amounts of herbs.

15 French-fry cutter This is the tool for those who prefer regimented fries to homely hand-cut ones. Push down the handle to force a peeled potato through the cutting grid. Alternate grids provide a choice of fry sizes, ranging from fat to thin.

16 Fish tweezer These tweezers alleviate the anxiety that sometimes accompanies eating fish. The 6-inch shafts terminate in rounded tips that are ridged on the inner sides. When clamped together, there is enough surface area to grasp and tweeze out lurking bones.

17 Fish scaler The underside of this solid aluminum tool is covered with close-set, sharp-edged studs that catch on the scales, lifting and ripping them out as you pass the scaler over the fish. If possible, descale your fish before gutting it—the fish will be firmer and rounder, and therefore easier to manipulate.

Cutting vegetables Vegetables cut into pieces of a uniform shape and size cook more evenly and improve the appearance of the finished dish. Most vegetables need to be cut in a particular way to suit the cooking method. With its wide, rigid blade, and gently curved cutting edge, the cook's knife is the best one to use for chopping, slicing, and dicing. A vegetable knife is better for peeling and slicing small vegetables and for gouging the eyes from potatoes. When cutting vegetables, always use a chopping board to protect your knife blades.

Chopping onions Peel the onion, leaving the root on, then slice in half from top to bottom. Lay each half cut-side down on a chopping board. Slice thinly lengthways, stopping short at the root (to hold the slices together), then slice thinly crossways. Discard the piece with the root. This method causes fewer tears than haphazard chopping – as the onion is held together during chopping, tear-inducing chemicals have less chance of escaping.

Slicing Chinese cabbage Remove any damaged outer leaves, then use a cook's knife to quarter or halve the cabbage from top to bottom. Place cut-side down and slice diagonally, beginning from the stem end. Angled slices not only look attractive, they also increase the area of cut edges exposed to the fat or liquid, thus reducing the time needed for cooking.

Dicing celery Using a cook's knife, trim the root and leaves from the stalks. Remove any tough strings with a swivel peeler. Lay the stalks on a board and slice them lengthways into three or four pieces of even width. Slice the wide part of the stalks near the root into shorter strips that are the same width as the other pieces. Lay all the strips flat and slice crossways to produce small squares.

Julienning carrots Use a vegetable knife or cook's knife to trim the carrots. Peel with a vegetable knife or peeler. With a cook's knife, slice a thin strip off one side so the carrot lies flat. Slice crossways into 2-inch pieces. Cut these lengthways into vertical slices about as thin as a matchstick. Stack the slices and slice again into thin strips, keeping the tip of the knife on the board as you rock the blade to and fro.

Cutting round vegetables into segments Depending on the vegetable's size, use a cook's knife or a vegetable knife. If cutting tomatoes, as shown here, use a very sharp vegetable knife or a serrated knife. Slice the vegetable in half from top to bottom. Place the halves cut-side down on a chopping board and slice in half again. Slice each quarter.

Ribbon-cutting leafy vegetables To make the leaves easier to roll, remove any thick stems by cutting through the ribs with a cook's knife, close to each side of the stem. If the leaves are very wide, cut them in half lengthways. Stack the leaves and roll them into a tight wad. Slice the roll crossways into strips of the required width.

summer squash salad

The recipe for this colorful summer salad was contributed by Anne Willan, founder of the famous La Varenne cooking school at Château du Feÿ in Burgundy, France, and one of the world's most trusted teachers. Her favorite tool is a black Matfer mandoline, which zips through the squash, cutting them into thin julienne sticks. The salad can be served at once, or after an hour or so, when the vegetables have wilted and softened slightly, though remaining crisp.

Serves 6 to 8 as an appetizer

Tools	Ingredients
cook's knife	4 small green zucchini, weighing about 1 lb. total.
mandoline	4 small yellow zucchini or other yellow squash, weighing about 1 lb. total.
bowl	juice of 2 lemons or limes
citrus juicer	2 shallots, finely chopped
small flat whisk	salt and freshly ground black pepper
	$1/2$ cup vegetable oil, such as sunflower
	2 tbsp. chopped fresh dill, or your favorite fresh herb
	fresh dill or other herb sprigs, to garnish

a

1 Trim the ends from the zucchini and cut them into 2-inch pieces.
2 Slice the pieces of zucchini lengthways on the julienne blade of a mandoline (a), rotating them as you slice, so that you come up with a julienne of the colorful outer peel and some of the flesh, but discarding the seeds and central core. Put into a bowl.
3 Make a vinaigrette dressing by whisking the lemon or lime juice with the shallots, salt, and pepper. Then whisk in the oil and add the herbs.
4 Toss the vegetable julienne with the dressing, taste, and adjust the seasoning. Divide between individual serving plates and garnish with a small sprig of dill or your chosen herb.

With its two handles and gentle rocking motion, the mezzaluna creates an even downward pressure that speedily reduces a mountain of fresh herbs to a mound, cutting cleanly through the leaves without bruising them.

tools for shearing and piercing

Scissors and shears cut cleanly, leaving no jagged edges. Many people prefer to cut with scissors rather than a knife, as the user exercises more muscular control when cutting, and the fingers are safely out of the way of the blade. A strong pair of kitchen scissors can be used for a range of tasks, such as cutting paper and string, trimming fins from fish and tips from artichokes, snipping herbs and bacon bits, and cutting dried fruit into bite-size chunks. If they are sturdy enough, kitchen scissors will even sever poultry, though poultry shears make easier work of it.

There are numerous occasions when food or certain types of containers need to be pierced, and there are a variety of tools designed to do the job. Basic piercing tools such as skewers and corkscrews are essential. However, some tools are so specialized they border on ridiculous; still others are so flimsily made they aren't worth kitchen drawer space. But there are surprises—you'll often find you get attached to a tool and it becomes indispensable.

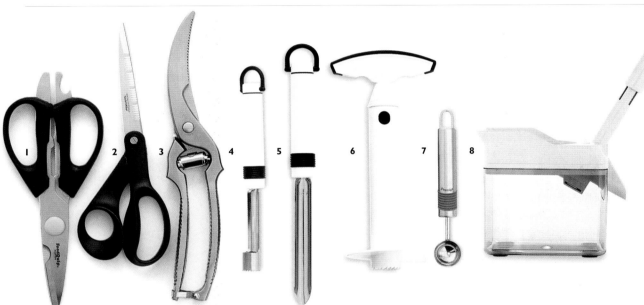

1 Kitchen shears The blades of these neat, all-purpose shears have a notch for cutting through poultry joints, while various parts of the handle can be used for opening jars and bottles, prying off lids, and as a screwdriver. The shears can be taken apart for washing and are dishwasher-proof.

2 Kitchen scissors These differ from household scissors in having longer blades, and one is usually serrated, making it easier to cut chicken or fish. The best scissors have forged blades and are made of stainless steel, which will not rust. Choose a pair with a screw rather than a rivet, so you can take the blades apart for cleaning or sharpening. Check handles for comfort.

3 Poultry shears These shears easily sever bones, sinew, and flesh. The blades are curved and pointed for intricate cutting, and a notch holds bones firmly during cracking. The strong spring kicks the handles apart, but it is a trap for raw poultry juices and needs thorough cleaning after use. A hook holds the handles together during storage.

Corers
To use a corer, push the circular cutting edge vertically through the middle of a fruit or vegetable, then withdraw it, bringing the core out in the cylinder. If you veer from the vertical, remnants of seeds and core will be left in the flesh, as they will if the core's diameter is greater than the cylinder's.
4 The shorter apple corer works reasonably well on apples and pears but is not suitable for anything longer.
5 To core zucchini, eggplant, and other elongated vegetables, you will need the longer vegetable corer.

6 Pineapple corer/slicer This tool does work, but it is probably worth buying only if you eat pineapples on a regular basis. Slice the top off the pineapple, then wind the slicer down over the core. When it reaches the bottom, pull upward and out will come a continuous spiral of pineapple flesh, devoid of unwelcome brown spots. The shell remains intact, ready for retro dishes such as pineapple boats.

7 Melon baller The melon baller is useful for occasions when neat spheres of melon are preferable to rough-cut chunks. To use the baller, press it deep into the flesh until juice flows from the hole in the base of the bowl. Then twist and remove. Some ballers have a smaller scoop at the other end, for removing shallow flesh close to the rind.

8 Cherry pitter There are times when the effort of pitting cherries is either worth it or necessary: for example, when making a cherry pie, when bottling and pickling cherries, or when feeding the very young. Though still laborious, the process is speeded up by a pitter, which also does the job neatly.

Load the cherries into the sloping tray, where they are funneled one by one into a stoning cradle. When you work the plunger, a metal rod pierces the fruit and removes the pit. The pit drops into the plastic container and the fruit falls into a bowl placed in front of the pitter. The tool also works reasonably well on olives.

Skewers

Skewers conduct heat through food, close flaps, and hold things in place. They are also used for testing cakes and poultry for doneness, and for piercing small citrus fruits and the skin of fatty birds to allow juice or fat to flow during cooking.

9 Bamboo skewers do not conduct heat as well as metal ones, but they are fine for small kabobs such as chicken satay. Though some cooks advise soaking bamboo skewers in water before use, I never do, and so far have not had to deal with a serious conflagration.

10 Kabob skewers are made of flat metal to prevent impaled food spinning round when you turn the skewer over. The most useful size is 10 to 12 inches, though there are longer and more flamboyant models for gaucho-style barbecues. Stainless-steel skewers are rustproof and easiest to keep clean.

11 Small round skewers, sometimes called poultry lacers, come in a range of sizes and are ideal for sealing poultry orifices and closing flaps. String can be threaded through the eye and used to close cavities more securely. The skewers are also useful for securing small parcels of food, such as paupiettes de boeuf. Butcher's skewers are used in much the same way.

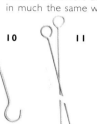

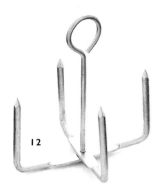

12 Potato baking spike Four metal spikes speed up baking by conducting heat to the center of the potato. There are drawbacks: baked-on starch is very difficult to remove from the spikes, the tool takes up a fair amount of oven space, and if you cook fewer than four potatoes, it becomes unbalanced. The spike is worth having, however, if you regularly bake potatoes for four people.

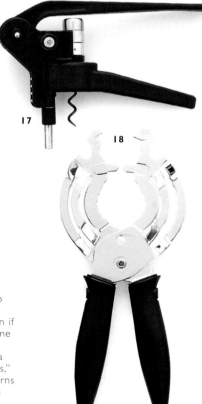

Can openers

A good can opener should work cleanly and continuously without coming to a halt halfway around the can. It should be effortless to use and feel comfortable in the hand.

13 The blue opener is easy to operate and is suitable for both right- and left-handed people. It is marginally less safe than some types, though, as it removes the entire rim of the can, leaving a clean but exposed sharp edge.

14 The chrome opener has an easy-to-grip butterfly handle and rounded black plastic inserts that protect the palms. The steel blade hooks over the rim of the can, leaving it in place once cutting is complete.

Corkscrews

Being a firm believer in the odd sip of wine while cooking, I regard the corkscrew as an essential tool. Even if you rarely imbibe, you will need wine for sauces and gravies.

15 This screw-pull corkscrew has a comfortable handle and an "endless," Teflon®-coated, spiral shaft that turns until the cork emerges. The shaft is open, with a well-rounded profile, enabling it to grip corks firmly (solid-shafted spirals do not grip as well).

16 Easy to use and reliable, this winged, stainless steel corkscrew has a self-centering frame that sits on the bottle rim, guiding the solid-shafted spiral through the cork. Turn the handle until the wings are fully raised, then press them down to remove the cork.

17 This state-of-the-art, lever-based model may look fearsome, but it's easy to use. With the lever fully open and the pincers gripping the bottle, swing the lever up and over to the closed position. This drives the screw into the cork. Swing the lever back to the open position and the cork will emerge.

18 Jar wrench Not strictly for piercing, this tool forces open unwilling lids and can cope with several sizes. Serrated inner edges create enough traction to grip and loosen the lid as you twist, while the sturdy non-slip handles allow you to use plenty of force. Various protuberances act as vacuum releasers, crown cap removers, and can piercers. The tool saves time, reduces frustration, and more than justifies its existence.

spatchcocked poussins
with rosemary-and-orange butter

The best way to grill whole birds is to cut out the backbone with poultry shears and press the carcass flat. They form a neat, flat shape that cooks evenly and quickly. Skewers keep the birds rigid when you turn them and help to conduct heat through to the thickest part of the thigh. Pushing herb butter under the skin keeps the flesh deliciously juicy.

Serves 4

Tools	Ingredients
mezzaluna or cook's knife	7 tbsp. unsalted butter, softened to room temperature
garlic press	2 tbsp. finely chopped rosemary
citrus grater	1 large garlic clove, crushed
mortar and pestle	finely grated zest of 1 small orange
small bowl	1/2 tsp. black peppercorns, crushed
fork	generous pinch of sea salt flakes
polyethylene chopping board	2 poussins, each weighing about 1 lb.
poultry shears or strong kitchen scissors	a few small rosemary sprigs, to garnish
4 flat metal skewers	
broiler pan with rack	

1 Combine the butter, rosemary, garlic, orange zest, peppercorns, and sea salt flakes, mixing well with a fork.

2 Put the birds on a polyethylene board, breast-side down. Using poultry shears or strong kitchen scissors, cut off the wing tips and lumpy joints at the end of the legs. Remove the backbone and pope's nose (the stubby tail protruberance) by cutting along the entire length of the bird, each side of the backbone (a).

3 Open out the birds and turn them breast-side up. Press down sharply with the heel of your hand to break and flatten the breastbone (b).

4 Separate the skin from the meat on the breasts, thighs, and drumsticks by carefully inserting your fingers between the skin and the flesh. Push knobs of the seasoned butter under the skin, spreading it as evenly as possible and molding it to the shape of the birds (c). Cover and leave in the refrigerator for at least 2 hours, or up to 24 hours.

5 When ready to broil, arrange the flattened birds so the drumsticks are turned inward, nestling close to the rib cage. Insert a metal skewer diagonally through the thigh, drumstick, and breast on one side and out through the wing on the other side (d). Insert a second skewer in the same way from the opposite side.

6 Heat the broiler until very hot. Place the poussins breast-side down on a rack in a clean broiler pan and position the pan 6 inches from the heat source. Broil for 15 minutes, then turn over and broil for another 15 minutes, or until the juices are no longer pink when you pierce the thickest part of the thigh.

7 Pull out the skewers—use oven mitts as they will be hot. Using clean poultry shears or kitchen scissors, cut each poussin into quarters, and arrange in a warm serving dish. Pour the buttery juices over, scraping up the sticky, tasty sediment from the bottom of the pan. Garnish with a sprig or two of rosemary and serve at once.

electric mixers and processors

These multipurpose machines not only chop and slice, but shred, beat, juice, whisk, and mix. They work at high speed, and are ideal for processing large quantities of ingredients quickly.

Although they are convenient, these items deprive cooks of some of the pleasure of preparing food. They also make it difficult to detect subtle physical changes in food while it is being processed. If you become reliant on a machine before you have learned to perform the tasks manually, you are unlikely to develop a true understanding of how and why ingredients behave as they do. That said, electric mixers and processors are worth their weight in gold if used judiciously. Having made the financial investment, make sure your mixer or processor earns its keep. You are more likely to use a machine if it is permanently within reach on the countertop, rather than hidden in a cupboard.

1 Stand mixer A classic mixer for the serious home baker, this machine has a 5-quart stainless-steel bowl that holds 5 pounds of ingredients. The rotary head "moves like Elvis," gyrating from the inside to the outside of the bowl in a series of circles, drawing in every scrap of mixture from the sides and base, and mixing it quickly, evenly, and thoroughly. The mixer has three basic attachments—a wire whip, a flat beater, and a dough hook—as well as numerous optional extras for a wide variety of tasks.

2 Food processor The food processor has become a near-necessity in the modern kitchen. The S-shaped blade effectively chops meat, vegetables, and fruit; makes bread crumbs; mixes dough; purées soups; and whisks dressings. Alternative cutting disks can be fitted to grate, shred, and slice.

Choose a processor with the largest container you can find. If the container sits on top of the motor, make sure it is not too tall to fit between the countertop and high-level cupboards. If space is tight, choose a processor with the container set next to the motor.

Though it is useful, the processor is not without drawbacks. Pieces of food tend to get stuck between the grating disk and the lid. It is not recommended for chopping herbs, and cannot be used for processing small quantities of food. If the mixture is not sufficiently liquid, the sides of the container will need to be continually scraped down.

3 Stick blender Even more compact than a handheld mixer, a stick blender is useful for blending small portions of food and frothing liquids— though for some tasks a whisk is just as good.

This model is sold with a useful mixing beaker, the diameter of which is slightly larger than that of the blades. This means that even a very small amount of food will come above the top of the blades, so it is ideal for making baby food. A whisk and a chopping attachment are also supplied.

4 Blender A kitchen classic, this deco blender has a powerful two-speed motor and a large, heat-resistant goblet. It blends, mixes, and juices, whizzing up the smoothest of smoothies, velvety sauces, soups, purées, and crushed ice. With its small diameter, the goblet keeps food within reach of the short, straight blades, so you don't have to keep stopping and stirring. Though a blender copes with smaller amounts of food than a processor, there must be enough to cover the blades. You will also need to add liquid; otherwise the food at the top will not be blended.

5 Juicer This machine transforms fruit and vegetables into pulp-free, health-promoting juice. Peeled fruit or vegetables are pushed into the filling shaft set over a rotating cutting disk. The disk reduces fibers to pulp, from which juice is extracted by centrifugal force through a fine mesh. The pulp remains behind while the juice drips into an integral container that also serves as a pouring pitcher. The only drawback is that the mesh needs a good scrub to clear it of pulp.

6 Multipurpose kitchen machine This revolutionary machine has a compact motorized base with a universal coupling device to which various attachments are easily fitted. The machine therefore combines several machines in one—the only drawback is its price. The basic model is supplied with a mixing bowl only, which has as accessories a lid, dough hook, double beater, and bowl scraper. The more expensive model comes with a blender and food processor, as well as the mixing bowl. Optional extras for both models include a grinder, a continuous shredder, and a grain mill.

7 Handheld mixer Lightweight and compact, the handheld machine is good for mixing relatively small amounts. The two overlapping steel beaters whisk egg whites into snowy clouds, whip cream, and emulsify sauces. You can also use the mixer for creaming butter and sugar, though the beaters get clogged up. Unlike the stand mixer, the handheld version allows you to control the position of the beaters. You can move them over the edge and base of the mixing bowl so everything is evenly mixed. A switch enables you to alter the speed while mixing.

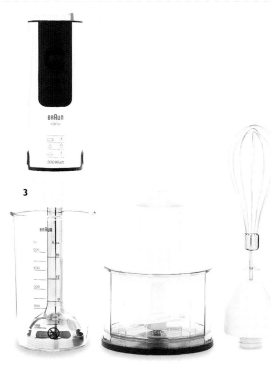

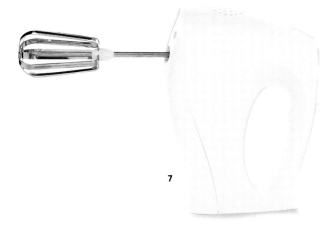

macadamia nut-crusted chicken breasts
with lemongrass-coconut emulsion

Contributed by award-winning chef and restaurant owner Charlie Trotter, this dish is rich and delicious, with sensual flavors that harmonize perfectly. The slightly wilted watercress is essential for cutting the richness of the macadamia nuts and balancing all the flavors. Use a handheld electric blender or mixer to froth up the sauce.

Serves 4

Tools	Ingredients
preparation bowls	2 cups coconut milk
cook's knife	1 cup milk
vegetable knife	1 cup chopped lemongrass
small saucepan	1 tbsp. rice vinegar
strainer	1 tbsp. lemon juice
citrus juicer	1 yellow bell pepper, halved and seeded
small bowls for prepared ingredients	1/2 cup julienned leek
	3 1/2 tbsp. peanut or sunflower oil
small roasting pan	
small skillet	1/4 cup julienned fresh gingerroot
large skillet	
perforated turner	4 skinned and boned chicken breasts, about 5 oz. each
handheld electric blender or mixer	salt and freshly ground black pepper
	1/4 cup chopped macadamia nuts
	2 cups watercress
	2 tbsp. shredded coconut, lightly toasted
	2 tbsp. snipped chives

1 Simmer the coconut milk, milk, and lemongrass in a small saucepan for 15 minutes. Strain through a strainer and pour back into the pan. Add the vinegar and lemon juice, and set the pan aside.

2 Meanwhile, broil the pepper until blackened. Peel off the skin and cut the flesh into matchstick strips; keep warm.

3 Plunge the strips of leek into a pan of boiling water. Bring it back to a boil and boil for a few seconds, then drain the strips and keep warm.

4 Heat 1 1/2 tablespoons of the oil in a small skillet. Add the ginger and fry for a minute or so until just golden. Remove from the pan and keep warm.

5 Season the chicken breasts with salt and pepper, and coat the tops with the nuts. Heat the remaining oil in a large, hot skillet, add the chicken and cook for 3 minutes on each side, or until cooked through. Transfer to a plate and keep warm.

6 Add the watercress to the pan in which you cooked the chicken. Cook it gently for 1 minute, or until wilted. Season to taste with salt and pepper.

7 Gently reheat the coconut emulsion, whisking with a handheld blender or mixer until frothy.

8 To assemble the dish, place some yellow bell pepper and leek in the middle of each serving bowl. Arrange some of the watercress over the vegetables and top with a chicken breast. Pour the emulsion around each bowl and sprinkle with the fried ginger and toasted coconut. Sprinkle the chives around the emulsion.

grinding
grating
and
crushing

mills, mortars, and grinders

These tools change the size and texture of ingredients, usually by abrading or crushing them between two hard surfaces in a closely confined space. A manual or mechanized rotary movement causes friction, which in turn produces the desired grounds, powder, or paste.

Using tools of this sort will immeasurably improve the flavor of your cooking, as they allow you to use raw materials rather than processed travesties. Think of the difference between freshly ground black pepper and the brown dust which passes for ready-ground pepper; or between the heady aroma of freshly ground spices and commercial curry powder.

Once crushed or ground, hard-coated ingredients such as coffee beans, peppercorns, and other spices release the volatile oils responsible for their distinctive flavors. When they are exposed to the atmosphere, the oils quickly oxidize and lose their pungency. Similarly, the fat in ground or grated Parmesan cheese will oxidize and become rancid before long, and a piece of meat will deteriorate rapidly once ground, because the much greater surface area increases its exposure to the atmosphere and to harmful organisms.

Tools for grinding and grating are therefore invaluable, enabling you to process ingredients at exactly the right moment for maximum flavor and minimum deterioration. Some tools not only grind but also act as storage containers, protecting the contents from the effects of light and air.

Spice mills

1 Liven up your curries with this fifties-style, black-and-chrome spice mill. Its rock-hard ceramic grinding mechanism is designed to cope with dried herbs and spices, as well as salt and pepper. The mechanism is fully adjustable for fine and coarse grinds. To maintain its jazzy good looks, however, the mill needs to be kept scrupulously clean.
2 Less glamorous but equally durable is the Crushgrind® spice mill. It, too, has a ceramic grinding mechanism, but there is no adjustment facility. Even so, the mill does its job remarkably well, and looks no less presentable, even after a stint in the kitchen. It is sold either as an empty container or filled with interesting spice blends.

3 Meat grinder A true kitchen classic, this cast-iron, hand-cranked grinder funnels meat into the spiral shaft of a revolving screw. From there, it is forced through rotating blades and finally through a perforated cutting disk. Alternate cutting disks can be fitted to regulate the fineness or coarseness of the end product.

Salt and pepper mills

4 These stylish, polished metal mills have a pull-down "laundry chute" refilling system that saves unscrewing and dismantling the top. The grinding mechanism, made from high-quality hardened steel, adjusts to produce a range of fine and coarse grounds.
5 Designed in a classic hourglass shape, these wooden mills have a chromed steel band for adjusting the grounds from fine to coarse. The stainless-steel grinding mechanism is constructed in such a way that there is no metal-to-metal contact, and it is therefore unlikely to wear out.

Choosing grinding tools

A pepper mill is a must. Choose one that holds at least three tablespoons of peppercorns, or you will be constantly refilling it. The best mills allow you to control the size of the grounds. Invariably sold as a pair with a pepper mill, a salt mill is useful if you live in a humid climate where caking is likely to be a problem.

No kitchen should be without a mortar and pestle. They perform a variety of tasks—grinding spices, making pesto, crushing garlic, for example—and so reduce the need for several different tools. If you like coffee, a coffee grinder will give you the unbeatable aroma and flavor of the drink made with freshly ground beans.

The other mills are a matter of personal choice. Whether you need them depends on how often you use an ingredient, and whether you prefer a mill or a grater. If you regularly use ground meat, for example to make burgers or terrines, it's worth buying a meat grinder. Yes, you have to clamp it to a table and wash the parts after use, but it is worth the effort. You can choose a decent cut of meat, there is no risk of contamination from meat that has previously passed through the grinder, and you can add your own seasonings.

6

Mill maintenance

O Use a pepper mill for pepper and a salt mill for salt. If you use salt in a pepper mill it will corrode the metal grinding mechanism. (A salt mill's mechanism is usually made from a noncorroding material such as nylon.)

O Lubricate the top of the spindle, where it meets the adjusting screw, with a drop of cooking oil. This will prevent rusting and keep the thread in good working order.

O Don't mill over open pans as steam causes rusting and dampens the grounds, which can clog up the mechanism. Mill into a large spoon or over a plate or piece of paper, then transfer the grounds into the pan.

O Keep mill bodies clean by wiping with a damp cloth. Rub wooden mills with vegetable oil occasionally to prevent the wood from drying out.

Coffee grinders

6 Working on the same principle as a blender, the two-armed blade of this electric mill pulverizes coffee beans in seconds. Though it is compact and easy to use, the grounds are uneven in size and you have to guess how long to whizz for. It is also noisy. Grinders that produce uniform grounds have grinding wheels rather than blades. They will satisfy purists, but are more complex to use and take up more space.
7 A more leisurely way of grinding beans is with a hand-cranked coffee grinder. As you turn the handle, the beans are fed into the hopper and through the metal grinding mechanism. The coffee grounds drop into the receiving drawer below. Based on a traditional design, this clear plastic grinder lets you see the beans being ground. It produces reasonable results, but the grounds are quite coarse.

Mortar and pestle

8 This solid metal mortar and pestle is designed primarily for grinding seeds and spices. The interior of the mortar has a flat base and straight, outwardly sloping sides, instead of the usual rounded bowl shape. The flat-tipped pestle mirrors the shape of the mortar and so maximizes the surface area available for grinding.
9 The ceramic mortar has a slightly abrasive, unglazed surface that grinds both dry and moist ingredients. Smooth mortars made from marble or glazed ceramic should have a ground surface on the inside; otherwise, dry foods will slide over the surface.
10 The Japanese mortar (suribachi) has a characteristically wide, shallow bowl, with an interior covered with unglazed ridges running in different directions. Used with the broad-tipped wooden pestle (surikogi), it efficiently grinds oily seeds and raw chopped fish or poultry to a coarse paste.

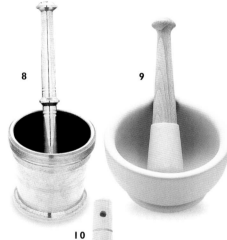

8   9

10

7   11   12

Nutmeg and Parmesan mills
These mills enable you to use up the last fragment of nutmeg or cheese without grating your fingertips.
11 The stainless-steel Parmesan mill will also grind nutmeg and cheese.
12 The chrome and acrylic nutmeg mill stores up to four extra nutmegs.

Pesto alla Genovese Bruising and pounding fresh basil leaves with a pestle beats any other method. Put 2 good handfuls of torn basil leaves, 2 mashed garlic cloves, 3 tablespoons of pine nuts, and a generous pinch of sea salt in a mortar and grind to a paste, moving the pestle around the mortar and crushing the ingredients against the sides. Add 8 tablespoons of freshly grated Parmesan cheese and 2 tablespoons of freshly grated pecorino Romano cheese, grinding until evenly mixed. Beat in 8 tablespoons of extra-virgin olive oil. This makes about ¹/₂ cup of pesto.

Garam masala Freshly ground garam masala (meaning "heating spices") lifts a curry from the mundane to the magnificent. A basic mixture includes an equal weight of cinnamon sticks, cloves, and black peppercorns, and a small amount of black cardamom seeds. Experiment with additional spices such as dried chilies, and fennel, cumin, and coriander seeds. For the best flavor, lightly toast whole spices and grind them to a powder just before use.

Pumpkin purée Cut peeled pumpkin or winter squash into chunks and simmer or steam until tender. Drain well and push through a food mill. The purée can be used to make pumpkin pie. Alternatively, for a colorful soup, dilute to desired thickness with good chicken stock. Add cooked black beans and some roasted mashed chili. Simmer gently to reheat. Pour into soup bowls and top with crumbled white cheese, pumpkin seeds, and a thin layer of pumpkin-seed oil or extra-virgin sunflower oil.

Fresh tomato juice Slice ripe, flavorful tomatoes in half, and push through a tomato press. For a thicker solution, allow the juice to settle before decanting, then pour off the clear liquid that appears on the surface. If you like, run the seeds and skins through the press again to extract more juice. Add the pulp to the first batch of juice.

coconut vegetable stew

Specializing in the light, home-style cooking of Kerala in southwestern India, Das Sreedharan's London-based Rasa chain of restaurants have revealed a very different side to Indian food. This colorful mixture of vegetables, cooked in a subtle blend of freshly ground spices, grated fresh coconut, and tangy yogurt, is typical of Keralan cooking. Known as "avial," it is a traditional festival dish, and no wedding or feast would be complete without it.

Drumsticks, or Indian asparagus, are podded seeds from a tropical tree. The pulp and seeds are sucked out of the cooked pods, rather like eating asparagus. To prepare drumsticks, string them like celery and cut into 1- to 2-inch pieces. They have an assertive flavor and some cooks like to parboil them for 10 minutes before proceeding with the recipe.

Green mango has a sour, fruity taste. Both green mango and drumsticks are available from good Asian food stores. If you have difficulty finding them, increase the quantity of the other vegetables, or substitute different ones. Instead of green mango, use a firm ordinary mango tossed with a pinch of citric acid or amchoor powder, available from good supermarkets.

Serves 4 as a side dish

Tools	Ingredients
mortar and pestle	1 tsp. cumin seeds
paring knife	1-inch piece fresh gingerroot, roughly chopped
vegetable peeler	
large saucepan	
wooden spoon	1 green chili, seeded and roughly chopped
grater	3 small carrots
colander	2 potatoes
	1 small green mango
	3¹/₂ oz. drumsticks, strings removed
	3¹/₂ oz. green beans
	20 curry leaves (optional)
	1 tsp. ground turmeric
	1 tsp. salt, or to taste
	8 to 10 tbsp. thick plain yogurt
	3 tbsp. coarsely grated fresh coconut
	few shreds fresh coconut, to garnish

1 Using a pestle and mortar, grind the cumin seeds, gingerroot, and chili to a paste with 1 tablespoon of water.
2 Slice the carrots, potatoes, and green mango into finger-shaped slices, ¹/₂-inch thick and about 2 inches long. Slice the drumsticks and beans into 2-inch pieces.
3 Put the carrots and drumsticks in a large, heavy-based saucepan with barely enough water to cover—about 1¹/₄ cups. Bring to a boil and simmer, uncovered, for 5 minutes, stirring occasionally to prevent sticking.
4 Add the potatoes and simmer over a medium heat, stirring now and then until nearly cooked, about 5 minutes.
5 Add the green beans, mango, and curry leaves, if using, and stir in the turmeric, salt, and spice paste. Reduce the heat and simmer for about 5 more minutes with the lid on, stirring occasionally until the vegetables are cooked.
6 Remove the vegetables from the heat and stir in the yogurt and coconut. Reheat gently if necessary but do not allow to simmer or the yogurt will curdle. Garnish with a few coconut shreds before serving.

graters

A grater is essentially a surface covered with rows of small, sharp cutting edges, and as such, it accomplishes the work of a knife in far less time and often with more uniformity. Some graters work in two directions, others in one only. When choosing a metal grater, make sure it is made of stainless steel; otherwise, it will rust. To clean stubborn debris from the cutting edges, rinse the grater under running water, then scrub with a nailbrush.

1 Porcelain grater This thick, flat porcelain grater (oroshigane) from Japan is a pleasure to use. Instead of perforations, it has rows of pyramidlike teeth angled in two directions. Used for gingerroot and daikon radish, the resulting pulp is moist, flavorful, and not at all fibrous. The grater can also be used for nutmeg.

2 Citrus grater Made of acid-resistant stainless steel, the lemon grater has very fine perforations. This enables you to grate the zest, or outer surface of the rind, without taking up any of the bitter pith.

3 Flat graters Flat graters are easy to store. It is better to buy two or three with different cutting surfaces, rather than a single flat grater with several grades, as the area of each will be small. The fine holes of the top grater are ideal for grating hard and semihard cheeses. The middle grater has very small toothed rectangular perforations that work in both directions. They reduce dense-fleshed fruit and vegetables such as apples and carrots to a sweet, moist pulp—perfect baby food or muesli topping. The third grater has coarser holes for grating root vegetables.

7 Rotary grater Ideal for thrifty cooks and for children, the rotary grater deals with scraps of cheese and can also be used for carrots, nuts, and chocolate. There is no risk of grating your fingertips as the food is pressed against the rotating drum by a wide covering plate at the end of the upper handle. Extra cylinders provide a choice of perforation sizes.

4 Box grater A box grater provides the greatest choice of cutting surfaces, ranging from very fine to coarse. It also has a slot for slicing cucumbers or shaving Parmesan. The rectangular base makes the grater self-supporting, which allows you to exert downward pressure more easily. The disadvantage is that the boxy shape makes it awkward to remove the grated pieces from the inside. This grater is also bulky to store and may not fit easily into a drawer.

5 Microplane® grater This state-of-the-art grater has rows of minute, ultrasharp blades that cut food precisely and cleanly with no shredding, tearing, or clogging. No pressure is required from the user. It has two drawbacks: the price, and the fact that you have to buy two graters if you want a choice of fine and coarse perforations.

6 Nutmeg grater Freshly grated nutmeg has a much better taste and aroma than the preground sort, so it is worth investing in a special grater or mill. The nutmeg grater has very fine perforations and a curved surface, both of which reduce the risk of grated fingertips.

Grating vegetables

Coarsely grating vegetables such as zucchini is an excellent way of insuring they cook evenly and fast, whether boiled, steamed, braised, or stir-fried. To stir-fry, tip the grated vegetables into a pan in which you have melted a knob of butter with a little olive oil. Stir-fry for 2 to 3 minutes, seasoning to taste.

Grating nutmeg
Nutmeg is at its most aromatic when freshly grated. Use a small, fine-holed grater and grate directly over the food. Here, a creamy rice pudding is prepared for the oven prior to baking. Cooked spinach, pasta tossed in cream, hot toddies, and cappuccino are also enhanced with freshly grated nutmeg.

Grating chocolate
Chocolate is messy to grate so the job is more easily done by remote control. Pop a small square into a rotary grater and grate directly over desserts such as ice-cream sundaes. A little goes a long way, so the tool is particularly useful for those who enjoy chocolate but need to watch their weight.

Grating fruit
Dense-fleshed fruits such as apples and pears are easier for some people to digest if they are very finely grated. A grater with sharp, fine blades, such as the Microplane®, makes light work of the firmest apple, and is ideal for grating fruit over muesli, or making fruit purées for older babies and toddlers.

mashers, crushers, and crackers

These invaluable tools break down the texture of raw or cooked food so that it becomes more palatable. They tenderize tough fibers such as those in raw meat, pierce thick skins, smash impenetrable nuts or lobsters, and produce delectable mashes and purées. These tools are not mere gadgets. They have stood the test of time and they do their job efficiently and well. Although their basic structure and function have not altered through the ages, many of these items are produced in stylish modern designs that complement today's kitchens.

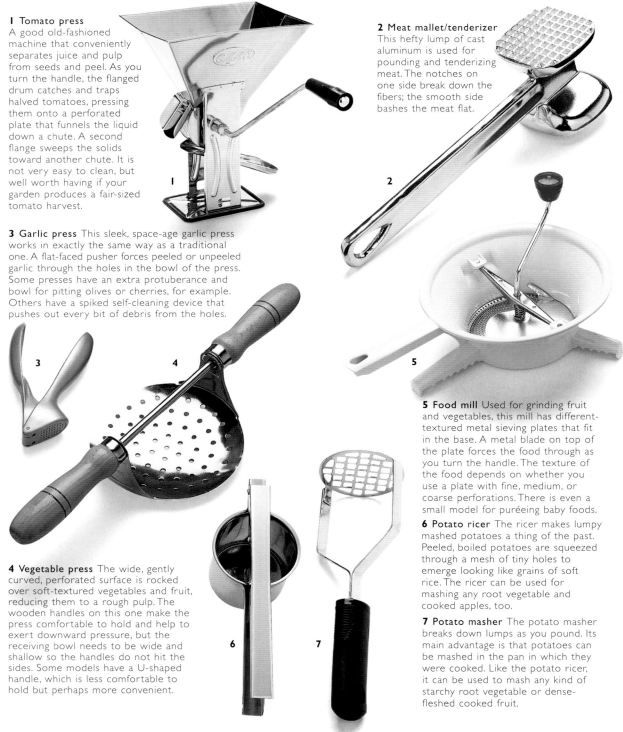

1 Tomato press
A good old-fashioned machine that conveniently separates juice and pulp from seeds and peel. As you turn the handle, the flanged drum catches and traps halved tomatoes, pressing them onto a perforated plate that funnels the liquid down a chute. A second flange sweeps the solids toward another chute. It is not very easy to clean, but well worth having if your garden produces a fair-sized tomato harvest.

3 Garlic press This sleek, space-age garlic press works in exactly the same way as a traditional one. A flat-faced pusher forces peeled or unpeeled garlic through the holes in the bowl of the press. Some presses have an extra protuberance and bowl for pitting olives or cherries, for example. Others have a spiked self-cleaning device that pushes out every bit of debris from the holes.

4 Vegetable press The wide, gently curved, perforated surface is rocked over soft-textured vegetables and fruit, reducing them to a rough pulp. The wooden handles on this one make the press comfortable to hold and help to exert downward pressure, but the receiving bowl needs to be wide and shallow so the handles do not hit the sides. Some models have a U-shaped handle, which is less comfortable to hold but perhaps more convenient.

2 Meat mallet/tenderizer
This hefty lump of cast aluminum is used for pounding and tenderizing meat. The notches on one side break down the fibers; the smooth side bashes the meat flat.

5 Food mill Used for grinding fruit and vegetables, this mill has different-textured metal sieving plates that fit in the base. A metal blade on top of the plate forces the food through as you turn the handle. The texture of the food depends on whether you use a plate with fine, medium, or coarse perforations. There is even a small model for puréeing baby foods.

6 Potato ricer The ricer makes lumpy mashed potatoes a thing of the past. Peeled, boiled potatoes are squeezed through a mesh of tiny holes to emerge looking like grains of soft rice. The ricer can be used for mashing any root vegetable and cooked apples, too.

7 Potato masher The potato masher breaks down lumps as you pound. Its main advantage is that potatoes can be mashed in the pan in which they were cooked. Like the potato ricer, it can be used to mash any kind of starchy root vegetable or dense-fleshed cooked fruit.

Nutcrackers

8 The hinged cone nutcracker is designed to accommodate a variety of nuts, both large and small. Furrowed gripping surfaces hold the nuts firmly in place while you crack them open.

9 The ratchet cracker does all the work for you. Simply place the nut between the ratchet and the top of the cracker and work the ratchet up with the lever until the shell cracks and falls apart.

10 The hinged pincer type requires some pressure to use, but the pleasure of extracting a whole kernel is worth the effort.

11 Lobster/crab crackers
Resembling lobster claws, these crackers work in the same way as hinged nutcrackers. The inside edges are ridged so you can grip unyielding lobster or crab claws firmly enough to crack them.

11

Citrus presses

12 This sturdy little, cone-shaped press is ideal for limes or small lemons. It squeezes out every drop of juice minus the seeds, and also squeezes out oils, giving the juice a more intense flavor. The press has a special silicone coating to prevent corrosion and discoloration from fruit acid.

13 A chrome body and an easy-to-grip, matte-black handle are an update on the time-honored wooden reamer. The tapered tip penetrates the flesh while the furrows crush and squeeze out the juice as the cone is turned. The reamer literally screws the juice out of half lemons or limes.

14 This glass lemon squeezer is of a traditional design. Place halved fruit over the dome and then press and twist to extract the juice. The pointed teeth arranged around the base of the dome prevent seeds from trespassing into the juice-collecting gutter.

15 This magnificent, tall, chrome citrus press is for serious juicing. Place half an orange or large lemon into the press, pull down the handle and the geared mechanism will extract every drop of juice from the fruit.

basic mashed potatoes

Although it seems simple, producing a mound of light, airy, lump-free mashed potatoes requires a little know-how. Variety of potato is important—use a floury type with a distinctive flavor (see Ingredients). Some cooks argue that it is better to boil potatoes unpeeled so water cannot penetrate and cause a waterlogged mash. I have tried boiling the same variety of potato with and without the skin, and cannot honestly detect any noticeable difference. When you are ready to mash, use a potato masher, or, for a creamier result, a potato ricer or food mill. Never use a food processor—unless you want wallpaper paste.

1 Put the potatoes in a saucepan with enough water to just cover them. Add 1 tablespoon of salt and cover with a tight-fitting lid. Bring to a boil, then simmer gently, with the lid in place, until tender—about 20 minutes. Drain well, peel if necessary and put back in the pan. Cover with a clean dishcloth for a minute or two to get rid of excess moisture.

2 For coarse-textured potatoes, mash the potatoes and butter with a masher (a). Season to taste with sea salt and freshly ground black pepper.

3 For smoother, fluffier potatoes, add some hot milk and, using a wooden spoon or balloon whisk, beat until you can beat no more (b). Add extra milk if needed.

Tools	Ingredients
saucepan with a lid	2¹/₄ lb. evenly sized floury
colander	potatoes such as Burbank Russet
clean dishcloth	or Yukon Gold, peeled or unpeeled
potato masher, ricer,	salt
or food mill	7 tbsp. butter, softened at room
wooden spoon or	temperature and cut into pieces
balloon whisk	²/₃ to 1¹/₄ cups hot milk

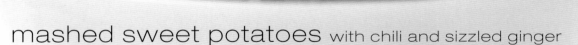

mashed sweet potatoes with chili and sizzled ginger

This flavorful variation on mashed potatoes is delicious served with spicy broiled chicken, lamb, or fish. You can use ordinary potatoes, of course, but sweet potatoes go particularly well with ingredients such as ginger and chili, since these ingredients share tropical origins.

Serves 4 as a side dish

Tools	Ingredients
vegetable peeler	2¹/₄ lb. orange-fleshed sweet
cook's knife	potatoes, peeled and cut into even-
saucepan with a lid	size pieces
colander	sea salt flakes and freshly ground
clean dishcloth	black pepper
potato masher	4 tbsp. chopped fresh cilantro
wooden spoon	2 tbsp. butter
medium skillet	1¹/₂ oz. piece fresh gingerroot, sliced
	into matchsticks, 1 inch long
	¹/₂ red chili, seeded and very finely
	chopped

1 Cook the sweet potatoes following step 1 of "basic mashed potatoes" above. They may need a little less cooking time than ordinary potatoes.

2 Mash the potatoes with a masher to break up the lumps. Season with sea salt and freshly ground black pepper and stir in the cilantro. Spoon into a warm serving dish.

3 Heat the butter in a skillet. When it is sizzling, throw in the ginger and chili. Fry for a minute or two until the ginger is golden. Pour over the potatoes, stir to partially mix, and serve at once.

mixing
and
whisking

bowls

Bowls are the nuts and bolts of kitchen utensils. After all, if you didn't have some sort of receptacle to mix, store, or serve in, how would meals ever be prepared? Bowls come in a wide range of materials: glass, copper, stainless steel, aluminum, enamel, ceramic, earthenware, melamine, and polyethylene. As with knives, you will need a variety of shapes and sizes for different tasks.

Bowls are vital for orderly, well-organized meal preparation. Get in the habit of preparing all your ingredients before you start to cook, and have them ready and waiting in appropriate bowls. Your "prep" bowls should include several small ones for ingredients like chopped garlic and ginger. Equally vital are three or four 1- to 4-quart bowls that can double up as serving bowls. If you regularly whisk egg whites or batters, you'll need a bowl that is deep enough to stop the mixture splattering your kitchen. You may want to treat yourself to a copper bowl for egg whites—your meringues will be unrivaled. Not absolutely essential, but useful nevertheless, is a big ceramic bowl for the occasional large mixing task such as a birthday cake.

3

5

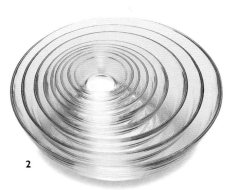

2

4

6

1 Basic glass bowl This plain glass bowl has a rolled rim for easy pouring. It comes with a plastic lid and is available in several sizes.

2 Duralex 9-piece set A bowl for every occasion, made of heat-tempered, oven- and microwave-proof glass. Use them for preparation, cooking, serving, and storing. This is a useful set to have if storage space is limited.

3 Stainless-steel bowls Stainless-steel is the ideal material for food preparation bowls as it is resistant to acid and is not tainted by smells. Pristine, shiny, and indestructible, these bowls are so elegant you won't want to put them away. Use them for preparation, serving, and storage.

4 Copper bowl An essential piece of equipment for meringue makers, this bowl transforms egg whites into billowing clouds of stable foam like no other bowl, thanks to the alchemy that takes place between copper and egg whites (see "miraculous meringue," page 49). The sloping sides and rounded base make for effortless whisking, while the generous diameter allows for rapid expansion of foam. The most useful size is about 12 inches in diameter.
Make sure your bowl has a rolled rim to keep its shape, and a hook so you can show it off on the wall.

5 Melamine bowl Rigid, tough, and practically unbreakable, melamine makes ideal bowl material. This one is gleamingly smooth, with a handy pouring lip and a rubber-rimmed base that prevents slipping. It is available in three sizes and a range of cheerful colors.

6 Ceramic bowl This traditional mixing bowl is made of glazed ceramic. The flattened area on the side keeps the bowl steady when it is tilted at an angle as you beat.

spoons

Together with bowls and knives, spoons are among the earliest and most basic kitchen tools. They are essential for any job involving mixing, and in many ways are simply a replacement for the hand. They stir, beat, scoop, and scrape, and can also be used as a measuring tool.

Wooden spoons are a must. They are strong, inflexible, and poor conductors of heat. You can leave a wooden spoon in a pan of simmering soup without fear of the handle heating up; nor will it bend or snap while you stir dense mixtures such as fruit cake. The curved back of a wooden spoon is perfect for pressing moisture out of cooked spinach, and for pushing soft fruit through a strainer. The handle can be used for molding shaped desserts such as tuiles or cannoli.

Though they may look somewhat crude, wooden spoons are subtly designed to perform a range of different tasks, so it is worth collecting a variety of sizes and shapes. Keep your spoons within easy reach of the stove. Those made from hardwoods, such as beech or boxwood, are strong and won't taint the flavor of your food. Pine or other softwoods can impart a resinous smell to food, and they also have a tendency to splinter and crack. Always wash and dry wooden spoons thoroughly after you use them, and preferably allow them to air.

A long-handled, large metal spoon is another must. The thin edge delicately cuts through airy mixtures such as whisked egg whites so they don't collapse as you fold in other ingredients. Use a metal spoon also for basting meat—the long handle will protect you from the heat—and for serving rice—the thin edge will not break up delicate grains as you scoop them up. Buy a spoon that you can hang on a hook, ready for its thousand and one uses.

Wooden spoons
1 A spoon with a straight edge and angled point fits snugly into the corners of a flat-bottomed pan, while the curved side copes with rounded pans. The blunt end can be used to move food around a sauté pan and dislodge sticky sediment from the base. This is a good spoon for making gravy.
2 This traditional wooden spoon is an essential tool. It is made of beech and has a beautifully curved oval bowl with thick sides.
3 This smaller basic wooden spoon is made of closely grained golden boxwood. The bowl is a similar shape to the beech spoon (2).
4 A long-handled spoon (at least 16 inches) is ideal for stirring continuously over extreme heat, when using a wok, for example, or for stirring polenta.

5 Metal mixing spoon With its perfect oval bowl and long handle, this metal spoon is of a high quality. Since the spoon is made from a single piece of metal, the handle will not come loose.

6 Wire mixing spoon This stylish spoon is used with rounded pans. The outer wire skims over any crust that may have built up on the pan base without incorporating it into the mixture. The thicker inner wire is strong enough for mixing, lifting, and turning. The spoon can also be used for whisking.

7 Scoop Useful for picking up dry goods such as flour or grains, the scoop has a straight-sided, deep bowl that holds a generous amount without spilling. Traditionally made of tinned steel, scoops such as this will rust if used for moist foods.

8 Insulated ice-cream scoop Made of seamless aluminum and filled with salt-based defrosting fluid, this tool is ideal for late-night ice-cream snacks. The tapered rim easily penetrates hard-packed ice-cream. It is not dishwasher-proof.

ladles and spatulas

Ladles are needed for transferring measured amounts of liquid or semiliquid food. They are invariably brought to the table, so buy a presentable one. To be avoided at all costs are ladles with painted wooden handles—they are guaranteed to flake or come loose. Make sure the bowl has a lip or continuous rolled edge for spill-free pouring. Hanging hooks are also useful.

Spatulas have virtually the same uses as spoons—they stir, mix, fold, and scrape; push things through strainers; and lift food from pans. Some cooks prefer a wooden spatula to a wooden spoon. One of the advantages of a spatula is that, being flat, it does not harbor clumps of unmixed food. You can also scrape it clean against the edge of the pan. Spatulas come in different materials and shapes. As with spoons, it's useful to have a selection for different tasks.

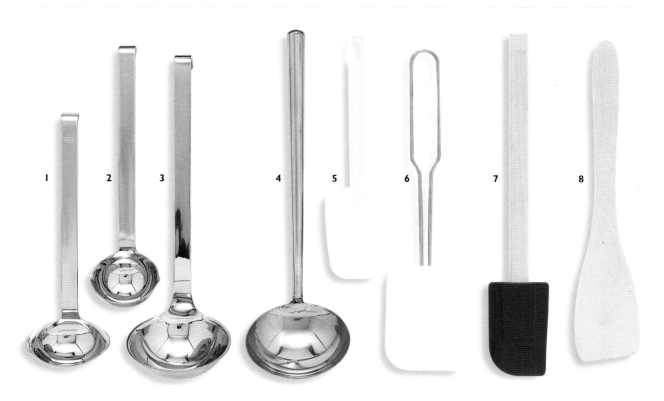

Ladles
1 Salad dressing ladle This ladle has a vertical handle that allows you to dip it into a tall, narrow container. The angle of the handle also makes it easier to pour with care over food that has been arranged on a plate. The bowl has a two-sided lip, designed for right- and left-handed use.
2 Portioning ladle The 2¹/₂-inch bowl has a pouring lip on each side that enables you to pour with precision, and is designed for right- and left-handed use.
3 Soup ladle A generous 3¹/₂-inch bowl will hold nearly ²/₃ cup of liquid—ideal for serving soup. The bowl has a continuous rolled lip to prevent drips, and the handle has a hanging hook that stops the ladle from becoming submerged if you leave it sitting in a large pot of liquid.
4 Chinese wok ladle The wide, shallow bowl is perfect for lifting, tossing, and turning the contents of a wok. The long handle distances you from the heat, and the 50° angle mirrors the contours of the wok, making the ladle more comfortable to use. Choose a stainless-steel ladle rather than rust-prone carbon steel.

Spatulas
5 Rubber spatula Shaped more like a spoon, this flexible spatula combines the benefits of a slightly concave bowl with straight edges and rounded corners. It will scrape clean a mixing bowl or pan without scratching.
6 Plastic spatula Available in three sizes, the flexible, fine-edged blade cleanly removes the very last scrap of mixture from a bowl, jar, or food processor bowl. One side deals with angled corners, the other with rounded.
7 Colored plastic spatula Similar in design and function, the colored spatula has the added benefit of being heat resistant. It will not melt or discolor, even at very high temperatures, nor will it damage nonstick cookware. It is available in a range of colors and sizes.
8 Wooden spatula The slightly angled end is useful for scraping mixtures out of corners and moving food around the pan. More importantly, the blunt edges will not scratch a nonstick surface, however firmly you scrape.

risotto with red wine and sausages

Australian food writer Jill Dupleix cannot cook without a wooden spoon: "It beats, it mashes, it stirs, it crushes garlic. It's a tasting spoon, a scraper, a risotto spoon, a porridge spoon, a salad server.... Wooden spoons are like dishcloths—no matter how many you have in the house, you will use them all." She puts her spoon to good use in this recipe.

Serves 4

Tools	Ingredients
medium nonstick skillet	10 oz. Italian pork link sausages, or coarse-grained pure pork sausages
cook's knife	1 tbsp. extra-virgin olive oil
large heavy-based sauté pan	2 tbsp. butter
wooden spoon	1 onion, finely chopped
small saucepan	1 1/2 cups arborio rice
ladle	3/4 cup plus 2 tbsp. red wine
grater	5 3/4 cups light chicken stock, preferably homemade
	2 tbsp. freshly grated Parmesan cheese
	sea salt
	freshly ground black pepper
	Parmesan shavings and small rosemary sprig, to garnish

1 Take the skin off the sausages and pinch the meat into a heated nonstick skillet. Fry the meat until crusty and golden, then drain off the fat and set the meat aside.

2 Heat the olive oil and half the butter in a heavy-based sauté pan. Fry the onion gently until softened but not browned. Add the rice and, using a wooden spoon, toss well until the rice is coated in the buttery onions. Pour in the red wine and bring to a boil, stirring.

3 Heat the stock in a small saucepan and keep it simmering. Using a ladle, add 1/2 cup of stock to the rice. Stir carefully and calmly with a wooden spoon over a medium heat. When the stock has been absorbed by the rice, add another 1/2 cup. From now on it is all in the timing. Add stock, a ladleful at a time, only when the previous stock has been absorbed by the rice. Keep the rice moving in the pan. If you go through a lot of stock quickly, the heat may be too high. If the rice doesn't absorb the stock easily, the heat may be too low.

4 After 20 minutes, add the sausagemeat and stir for another 10 minutes until the rice is cooked but not soft, and there is a general creaminess to the sauce; it should be neither soupy nor dry.

5 Turn off the heat. Add the Parmesan, the remaining butter, and sea salt and freshly ground pepper to taste, and stir it through. Cover and leave to rest for 3 to 4 minutes before serving. Garnish with a rosemary sprig and a few Parmesan shavings. Serve with plenty of red wine on the side (to drink, naturally).

whisks

Air is the least recognized—but one of the most fundamental—ingredients in cooking, and, as we need a means of incorporating it into food, the whisk could rightly be called the most fundamental of tools.

A whisk works by cutting at high speed through egg whites, batters, sauces, and other ingredients, not only incorporating air but also performing other vital functions. A whisk smoothes out lumps and uneven concentrations. It breaks down fat globules so they emulsify with nonfat liquids—oil and vinegar in a salad dressing, for example. A whisk also "denatures" proteins—think of egg whites and the way a viscous mess miraculously turns into a frothy cloud. In this case, the whisk cuts through interwoven strands of protein molecules in unbeaten egg white, effectively chopping them into tiny pieces and introducing air at the same time.

There are a number of shapes and sizes of whisks, designed for a variety of jobs. If choice is restricted, however, a balloon whisk and possibly a small flat whisk are the ones to go for. Choose ones made of stainless steel rather than tin plate, which is likely to discolor and rust. The handle should be comfortably thick and sit well in the hand, and, in the interests of hygiene, should be well sealed at both ends. The wires should be firmly welded in place.

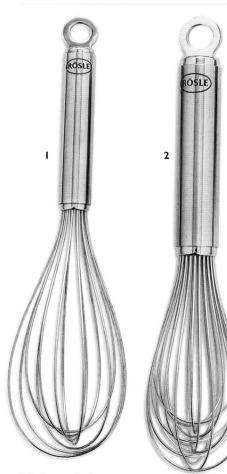

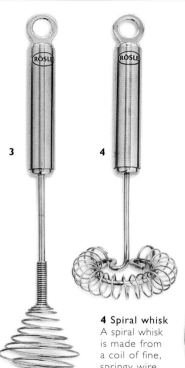

1 Balloon whisk
The balloon whisk's slightly flexible wires will effectively aerate anything from egg whites to heavy cream. Their bulbous shape increases the area that is in contact with the mixture, so the more wires the better.

2 Egg whisk The egg or sauce whisk is designed to mix, emulsify, and aerate egg-based sauces. More elongated and rigid than a balloon whisk, the wires cut through egg proteins in a hollandaise sauce, for example, preventing coagulation and curdling.

3 Twirl whisk
Also called a whip, this is made from one piece of coiled wire, which gives it greater flexibility. Though the shape makes it useful for working into corners and around the base of a container, it is not as efficient as a balloon or egg whisk. It is good for whisking in slim containers, however.

4 Spiral whisk
A spiral whisk is made from a coil of fine, springy wire, looped around a circular wire frame. It can be used in a small amount of liquid, so it is invaluable for whisking sauces in shallow pans. This whisk also incorporates mixture from around the edge of the mixing bowl.

5 Jug whisk
Not essential but nevertheless useful, the long jug whisk comes in handy for whisking things in narrow glasses, measuring jugs, and cocktail shakers.

6 Flat whisk
This whisk is excellent for mixing small amounts, or for beating a single egg yolk, stirring delicate items, or mixing herbs into cream.

spicy shrimp crêpes with cilantro sauce

For successful crêpes, use a balloon whisk, which effectively mixes and aerates the batter, and smooths out lumps. Do not overbeat or your crêpes will be tough. Use a small, heavy pan that conducts heat evenly and does not stick. A crêpe pan or a well-seasoned omelete pan is ideal.

Makes 8 crêpes

Tools	Ingredients
sieve	²/₃ cup unbleached all-purpose flour
mixing bowl	pinch of salt
balloon whisk	I egg, plus I egg yolk
small measuring	I¹/₄ cups milk
jug	I tbsp. vegetable oil or melted butter
paring knife	I¹/₂ tsp. ground turmeric
cook's knife or	vegetable oil, for frying
mezzaluna	*For the sauce:*
ladle	I garlic clove, finely chopped
7¹/₄-inch	3 tbsp. chopped cilantro
nonstick crêpe	7 oz. whole milk yogurt
pan	¹/₂ tsp. freshly ground cumin
turner	sea salt and freshly ground black pepper
waxed paper	*For the filling:*
small skillet	I tbsp. vegetable oil
aluminum foil	¹/₂ onion, finely chopped
	2 tsp. red Thai curry paste
	I¹/₂ cups canned chopped tomatoes with juice
	24 large peeled tiger prawns or jumbo shrimp
	I tbsp. lemon juice
	2 tbsp. chopped fresh cilantro

1 Sift the flour and salt into a bowl. Make a well in the center and add the egg and extra yolk (a). Add half the milk and whisk well (b). Continue to whisk, gradually adding the rest of the milk, until the batter is smooth. Pour into a small measuring jug and set aside.

2 Mix together all the ingredients for the sauce. Leave to stand to allow the flavors to develop.

3 Whisk the vegetable oil or melted butter into the batter along with the turmeric. Heat enough oil to lightly film a 7¹/₄-inch skillet. When the oil is hot but not smoking, quickly add a small ladleful of batter, tilting and turning the pan as you do so (c). Fry quickly over a medium-high heat until set on top and brown underneath. Using a fish turner or quick flip of the pan, turn the crêpe and cook until the underside is brown.

4 Transfer the crêpe to a plate and keep warm. Repeat, using the remaining batter, to make seven more crêpes. Stack the crêpes with a sheet of waxed paper between each one. Cover with foil and keep warm.

5 To make the filling, heat the oil in a small skillet and gently fry the onion until golden. Add the curry paste and stir-fry for I minute. Stir in the tomatoes and season with salt to taste. Simmer for I to 2 minutes. Add the shrimp, lemon juice, and cilantro. Simmer for a few minutes until the shrimp are thoroughly heated through.

6 Fold the crêpes in half, and then in half again to make quadrant-shaped cones. Spoon the filling into the top pocket. Arrange in a warm serving dish or on individual plates, and top with a spoonful of sauce.

Crisp and chewy on the outside, soft as clouds within, meringues have been known to induce cries of ecstasy even from those who are normally unenthusiastic about desserts.

Sabayon sauce Use a large balloon whisk to make a light, sweet sauce to serve with hot pies and puddings, or to spoon over summer berries. Put 3 large free-range egg yolks, 1/4 cup of superfine sugar, and 7 tbsp. of white wine, preferably sparkling, into a large heatproof bowl. Set this over a saucepan of gently simmering water. Beat the mixture steadily until it increases in volume and becomes a firm but light and creamy foam that forms a trail when the whisk is lifted. **Serves 4.**

Mayonnaise Use an egg whisk or sauce whisk to make creamy mayonnaise for salads and dips. Put 2 free-range egg yolks, 1/4 teaspoon of sea salt, 1/4 teaspoon of mustard powder, a little freshly ground black pepper, and 1/2 teaspoon of olive or sunflower oil into a medium-size bowl. Beat until smooth, then beat in another 1/2 teaspoon of oil. Continue adding oil in tiny amounts, increasing the flow as the mixture thickens. You will need a total of 1 cup of oil. Finally, mix in 1 tablespoon of white-wine vinegar and 1 tablespoon of warm water. Check the seasoning. To make aïoli, add 5 to 6 garlic cloves, pounded to a paste with a little sea salt, at the start and omit the vinegar. **Makes about 1 1/2 cups.**
Note: This contains raw eggs, which can be hazardous to young children, pregnant women, and the elderly.

sieving
and
straining

sieves, sifters, and dredgers

These tools refine the texture of food. They smooth lumps and coarse particles from free-flowing powders such as flour or confectioners' sugar; and they indirectly lighten mixtures, because the process of sieving or sifting helps to incorporate air as the powder floats down into the receiving bowl.

Sieves are additionally used to separate solids from liquids, as in draining peas, or to alter the texture of food. For example, hard-boiled egg yolk can be transformed into a mimosalike garnish by pushing it through a fine-meshed sieve. Raspberries can be divested of their seeds in the same way. A sieve is also useful for rescuing lumpy gravy or a béchamel sauce that is not as smooth as it should be—place the sieve over a clean saucepan, pour the mixture into the sieve, and smooth out the lumps by pressing with the back of a wooden spoon.

A sieve should sit comfortably over the receiving container. Conical sieves work best with tall containers; bowl-shaped sieves are best used with bowls. The container needs to be large and deep enough to accommodate both the depth of the sieve and the depth of the ingredients once sieved. Don't sift dry powder in a damp sieve as you'll end up with paste. Nor is it advisable to sieve seedy or fibrous food through an ultra-fine sieve—it will be very difficult to clean. If you do need to clean fibrous material from a sieve, hold it under running water with the inside facing down and scrub the outside of the sieve with a nail brush. Turn the sieve bowl-side up, scrub the inside, and rinse again.

1 Dredgers A dredger is used to store and dispense flour (large holes) or sugar (small). Turn the dredger upside down and shake it like a salt cellar. The top unscrews for filling. When refilling a sugar dredger, take care not to let the crystals stick to the thread. They will cause problems with screwing and unscrewing.

2 Drum sieve Used in India and known as a "tami" in France, this sieve has a closely woven mesh stretched tightly over its circular frame. Frames come in wood, plastic, or metal, and in a wide range of diameters. Meshes are made of nylon, silk, or metal, and are usually interchangeable. Depending on the closeness of the weave, the sieve removes lumps from powders and coarse particles from spices and grains. A drum sieve is useful for sieving large amounts, as ingredients pass through a flat mesh more quickly than a concave one. However, dry ingredients tend to randomly sprinkle over a wide area, which may be a problem if you want to confine them to a small space.

3 Flour sifter This spring-set sifter aerates clumpy flour to a light, uniform consistency. It has a fine-meshed base with spokes set above it that agitate the flour as you press the trigger in the handle. The process is somewhat laborious, so the tool is suitable for sifting small quantities of flour only. Try to refrain from washing it, as a damp sifter turns flour to paste. It will remain clean enough if you store it in a plastic bag in a cupboard or drawer.

Choosing sieves Essential are two or three medium-to-large bowl-shaped sieves; then you will always have a dry one ready for use. A large sieve, measuring about 10 inches in diameter, is worth having for sieving any reasonable quantity of flour or confectioners' sugar. If the sieve is too small, the powder tends to either spill over the edge of the sieve or float into the atmosphere; a sieve with a generous-size bowl will keep it in place. A couple of smaller sieves, about 4 to 4½ inches in diameter, are useful for directing powder or liquid into a narrow-necked container such as a measuring jug. Essential for sieving soft fruits or removing seeds from citrus juice is a fine-meshed sieve made of nylon, which, unlike metal, does not react with the acid in the fruit.

When buying, ensure that the sieve has an ear or lip to rest on the edge of the container. Also, check the strength of the mesh, as this will take the brunt of the pressure when you work foods through it. The weakest point is the base of the bowl, which may eventually wear out.

4

4 Nylon sieve A nylon sieve is noncorroding and therefore preferable for sieving acidic foods that might be tainted by metal. It is molded from one piece of plastic, and therefore has no joints to break or work loose. This sieve will last a lifetime, so choose a color you can live with.

Bowl-shaped sieves The very fine mesh of these attractive stainless-steel sieves are ideal for sifting flour, confectioners' sugar, and other fine powders.
5 The larger sieve can also be used to drain small amounts of vegetables.
6 The small sieve is useful for sprinkling confectioners' sugar over cakes, as it enables you to aim more accurately.

5   6   7

7 Chinois and pestle Also called a "bouillon strainer," this conical sieve funnels liquids downward into the tip for more accurate pouring. The ultrafine, twill-like mesh clears stocks of every sediment and strains sauces to velvety smoothness. The sieve is sturdily made with a wide top band to which are welded the handle, hook, and frame. The frame protects the mesh from damage.

The pestle is tapered to fit into the bottom of the sieve. Use it to extract flavorsome juices from solid matter, and to produce a very thin purée from softened vegetables—great for thickening and flavoring sauces.

strainers and skimmers

Though the terms "sieve" and "strain" may be used interchangeably, a strainer usually has a coarser mesh than a sieve, or holes. It is used mainly to separate solids from liquids. Skimmers remove sediment, fat, and scum from the surface of liquids.

A colander is essential. If you cook for crowds, make large amounts of stock, or regularly make pasta for four or more people, you will need one at least 11 inches in diameter. It should have feet or a solid base so both your hands are free for lifting the pan from which you are pouring the food. Smaller colanders do not need feet, but should have a sturdy lip and a handle for resting on the receiving utensil. The base should be fairly flat so food at the bottom is not crushed. To drain efficiently, a colander needs a generous number of holes that are reasonably-sized but not so large that peas slip through them. Make sure they are evenly distributed and come up the sides of the colander.

If you enjoy properly dressed salads, a spinner for drying leaves is another must. A collapsible wire basket is attractive, but does not do as good a job as an enclosed spinner that strains by centrifugal force. Some spinners have a perforated base—the idea being that you hold it over the sink, and spin and drain in one go. I usually end up showering my feet because I forget the base is perforated, so I prefer a spinner with a solid base.

Other essential straining tools are a large perforated metal spoon (look for one that is made from a single piece of metal) and, if you make tea with loose leaves, a tea strainer.

1 Cheesecloth A lightweight cloth that filters out fine sediment from stocks or clarified butter. Place a large piece inside a sieve or colander and pour the liquid through. It is light-textured enough to wrap around soft food such as yogurt cheese (see page 58) to mold it or hold it in shape.

Colanders
2 This well-designed stainless-steel colander has wide grips for lifting or for resting on a bowl, a solid stand, widely spaced holes, and a large hole for hanging. The flat base helps prevent food from being crushed. It is available in diameters ranging from 6 1/2 to 11 inches. Buy the largest one possible.
3 Although you can set the long-handled colander down, you are more likely to hold it with one hand and the pan from which you are pouring in the other. It is therefore best used for straining manageable amounts rather than the contents of a vast and heavy pot. A diameter of 7 1/4 to 8 inches is a useful size to have.
4 The enameled colander is the kind of utensil you can become inexplicably attached to. Traditional in appearance, it has three sturdy feet to hold it steady, plenty of perforations, and two U-shaped handles that won't slip or get hot. The enamel may chip in time, but that adds to its charm.

3

2

4

5 Pan drainer Shaped like a crescent moon, the stainless-steel strainer drains small-to-medium amounts of pasta or vegetables directly from the pan. It is held in place by a rim that attaches to the pan edge, and will fit a range of pan sizes.

6 Perforated spoon This vital utensil simultaneously strains and lifts small amounts of food from pans. Cooking juices, water, or fat drains off through the perforations.

7 Tea strainer Made of stainless steel, this smart little strainer has a very fine mesh for straining freshly brewed tea or coffee. The wire ear and handle allow you to rest it on your cup—useful if you need two hands to lift a large teapot.

8 Conical strainer This coarse-meshed strainer is handy for straining into a small or narrow container such as a gravy boat or sauce jug. It is available in four diameters ranging from 3½ to 8 inches.

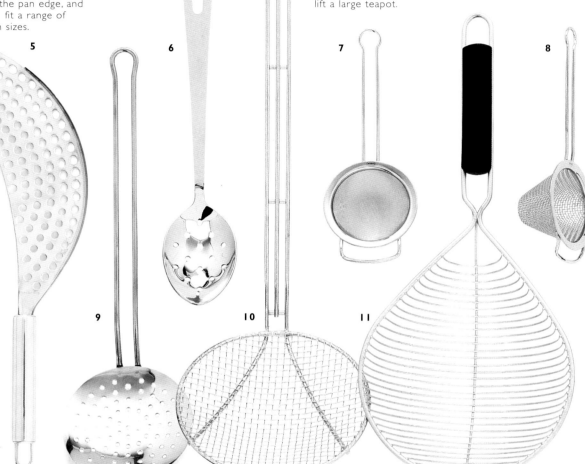

9 Perforated skimmer The extra-wide, flat bowl skims froth and skin formed by impurities from the surface of stews and stocks. The skimmer can also be used for lifting and draining dumplings or gnocchi.

10 Wire skimmer This skimmer is designed for removing fried food from deep fat. The wires allow fat and small bits of sediment to quickly drain away.

12 Wire shaker Charming though it may be, there is no avoiding the fact that water sprays everywhere when you whirl this shaker around. Shaking it gently over the sink does not do the job effectively, and it is best used in the garden.

13 Salad spinner This superbly designed spinner is effortless to use. Unlike many other models, you don't have to cradle it in your arm—just place it on the countertop and pull the string. Centrifugal force presses the leaves against the internal meshed basket, driving water off into the outer container. The clear perspex outer container is good-looking enough to use as a salad bowl—once you've emptied the water. There is a more expensive version with a stainless-steel bowl.

11 Noodle/pasta scoop This simply designed wire strainer has a pleasingly deep and generous bowl that is ideal for scooping up and straining gnocchi, dumplings, and stuffed pasta or noodles such as ravioli, wontons, or pot stickers.

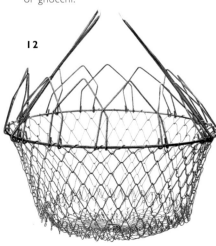

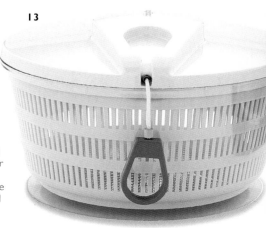

yogurt cheese

This is a type of soft cheese popular in the Middle East and India. Yogurt is tied up in cheesecloth and left to strain for 6 to 36 hours—the shorter time making for a very soft, mild cheese and the longer a denser cheese with a more pronounced flavor. The end result is similar to cream cheese, but lighter in texture and lower in fat.

Yogurt cheese is wonderfully versatile, and combines well with either sweet or savory ingredients. For a tasty snack, spread it on crackers or toast, or, if it is quite soft, serve it as a dip with crisp vegetable sticks. For a quick and simple dessert, sweeten yogurt cheese with a dusting of sugar or a slick of honey, fruit purée, or syrup.

Mixing yogurt cheese with chopped fresh herbs is also delicious. Finely chopped scallions, green chili, or a little grated ginger can be mixed in, too. Firm yogurt cheese can be shaped into balls or logs and then rolled in sesame seeds, or coarsely ground black or green peppercorns. Serve with flat bread and olives.

basic yogurt cheese

The type of yogurt used will affect the flavor, texture, and amount of cheese produced. Plain yogurt gives off a fair amount of liquid, so the weight of cheese produced is slightly less than you would get from set yogurt, which is thicker. Bio, or live, yogurt is naturally mild in flavor, so will produce a mild-tasting cheese, whereas cheese made from yogurt that is high in lactic acid has a sharp, acidic flavor. Organic whole milk yogurt produces a particularly delicious cheese—mild in flavor, with a slightly grainy texture.

Enough for 3 to 4 servings

Tools	Ingredients
three 20-inch squares cheesecloth	4¹/₂ cups plain yogurt
colander	
string	
large deep bowl	
wooden spoon	

1 Moisten three squares of cheesecloth and use to line a colander, draping the corners over the sides.

2 Spoon the yogurt into the center of the cheesecloth. Gather up the four corners and twist to squeeze the yogurt into a ball.

3 Tie tightly with string and fasten onto the handle of a wooden spoon. Rest the spoon over a deep bowl so the yogurt hangs free (or use a shallower bowl with supports on either side, as shown here). Make sure there is a gap of at least 2 inches between the bottom of the cheesecloth and the base of the bowl. Leave in a cool place to drip for 6 to 36 hours.

yogurt cheese
with pomegranates, spiced sugar, and pistachios

In this simple but exquisite dessert, jewel-like pomegranate seeds and a sprinkling of green pistachios adorn a sweetly perfumed mound of yogurt cheese. The yogurt should be quite soft and mild, so drain it for about 12 hours.

Serves 4

Tools

small bowl
cook's knife
wooden spoon
paring knife

Ingredients

6 tbsp. pistachio nuts

yogurt cheese, 1 1/2 cups when drained, made with organic whole milk yogurt and drained for about 12 hours (see opposite)

1/2 tsp. rose water

3 tbsp. spiced sugar (see below)

1 large pomegranate

1 Put the pistachio nuts in a small bowl and cover with boiling water. Leave for 5 minutes, then slip off the skins. Chop the nuts roughly and set aside.

2 Beat the yogurt cheese with the rose water and spiced sugar. Divide the mixture between four serving bowls.

3 With a small sharp knife, cut the pomegranate skin lengthways into four segments, taking care not to puncture the juicy seeds inside. Break the pomegranate in half, and then into quarters. Bend the skin back to release the seeds, discarding any bits of membrane. Sprinkle the seeds over the yogurt and top with the pistachios.

Spiced sugar Using a mortar and pestle, grind to a powder 6 cloves, 1/2 teaspoon of peppercorns, seeds from 15 green cardamom pods, and 1/2 teaspoon of fennel seeds. Mix with 1/2 teaspoon of ground cinnamon. Stir the spices into 1 3/4 cups sugar, mixing well. Keep it in a screwtop jar and use as needed.

pumpkin and girolle soup

This recipe was contributed by the dazzlingly inventive Alain Ducasse, the only chef with six Michelin stars, and mentor to a new generation of chefs who are changing the face of French cooking. A fine-meshed chinois is used to purée the pumpkin for this delicious soup, which is ladled over tiny sautéed girolle mushrooms and topped with crisp lardons and whipped cream.

Serves 4

Tools	Ingredients
cook's knife	3 tbsp. olive oil
large saucepan	3 1/4 cups fresh pumpkin, peeled, seeded, and cubed
wooden spoon	
chinois and wooden pestle	I small onion, finely chopped
	2 cups chicken stock (see page 62)
deep bowl	6 tbsp. unsalted butter
paring knife	1/2 tsp. fine sea salt, or to taste
mezzaluna	1/4 tsp. freshly ground black pepper, or to taste
medium skillet	
utility knife	just under 1/2 cup heavy cream, lightly whipped until it just forms peaks
small saucepan	
small strainer	
small frying pan	just under 1/2 cup heavy cream, whipped until it holds firm peaks (optional)
paper towels	
medium saucepan	*For the garnish:*
balloon whisk	I tbsp. olive oil
electric mixer	8 oz. small girolle mushrooms, trimmed and cleaned
	I shallot, finely chopped
	2 tbsp. unsalted butter
	2 tbsp. finely chopped chives
	3 oz. slab bacon or pancetta, cut into 1/2-inch cubes (lardons)
	4 leafy sprigs fresh chervil

1 In a large saucepan, heat the oil over medium-high heat. Add the pumpkin and onion, and stir to coat with oil. Reduce the heat to medium-low and cook until the pumpkin softens and the onions are translucent, about 5 minutes. Pour in enough stock to cover, and cook until the pumpkin is very soft, 10 to 15 minutes.

2 Remove from heat and let cool slightly. Set a chinois sieve over a deep bowl then pour the mixture into the sieve, pressing the vegetables through the mesh with a wooden pestle. Put aside the sieved liquid.

3 To prepare the garnish, heat the oil in a medium skillet over medium heat. Stir in the mushrooms and shallot and cook, stirring often, until the mushrooms give off their liquid and it evaporates. Add the 2 tablespoons of butter, then the chives. Stir in and remove from the heat.

4 Put the lardons in a small saucepan and cover with cold water. Bring to a boil over high heat, reduce the heat to medium-low, and simmer for I minute to blanch and remove some of the salt. Drain and rinse briefly in cold water. Drain again and pat the lardons dry. Sauté the lardons in a small skillet until they are brown and crisp. Transfer to paper towels to drain.

5 To finish the soup, combine the pumpkin mixture with the remaining chicken stock in a medium saucepan. Bring to a gentle boil, then stir in the 6 tablespoons of butter, and the salt, pepper, and lightly whipped cream.

6 Pour the mixture into the bowl of an electric mixer and beat on medium speed until smooth and creamy. Adjust the seasoning to taste.

7 Pour into a warmed soup tureen. Divide the mushroom mixture among four warmed soup plates. Spoon in the pumpkin soup. Sprinkle on the lardons, then, if you wish, place a dollop of thickly whipped cream in the center of each serving. Garnish with sprigs of chervil and serve immediately.

ramen with pork and vegetables

This hearty noodle soup was contributed by leading Japanese food writer Emi Kazuko. Ramen are Chinese-style noodles served in soup with various toppings. The dish is one of the most popular in Japan, where there is a ramen museum, a ramen village, and even ramen appreciation clubs. These noodles can be bought from health food shops and good supermarkets. To make this dish, you will need strainers of various sizes for straining the vegetables, meat, and noodles.

Serves 4

Tools	Ingredients
medium skillet	*For the braised pork:*
medium saucepan	7 oz. pork tenderloin, in one piece
paring knife	
small and medium strainers	1 tbsp. vegetable oil
	2 1/4 cups chicken stock
cook's knife	5 tbsp. shoyu (Japanese soy sauce)
paring knife	
small bowl	2 tbsp. sugar
utility knife	1/2 tsp. salt
large saucepan	2 scallions, sliced into 2-inch pieces
colander	
	1 1/4- to 1 1/2-inch square piece of fresh gingerroot, roughly sliced
	For the ramen:
	3 1/2 oz. spinach, trimmed
	1/2 cup bean sprouts
	salt and freshly ground black pepper
	7 oz. dried ramen (Japanese noodles)
	4 1/2 cups chicken stock
	1/2 pork or beef bouillon cube (optional)
	3 1/2 oz. baby corn, cooked
	1 scallion, finely chopped, to garnish
	rayu, or chili oil (optional)

1 Brown the pork on all sides in the oil over medium-high heat to seal the meat. Remove from the heat.

2 Put all the other ingredients for the braised pork in a medium saucepan and bring to a boil. Add the browned meat and simmer, covered, for about 1 hour. Leave the meat to cool in the liquid.

3 Lightly boil the spinach, then drain under cold running water for a few seconds. (This makes the green color bright.) Squeeze out excess water with your hands, and chop into bite-sized pieces.

4 Place the bean sprouts in a bowl and pour boiling water over them. Leave for 5 minutes, then drain. Season with a pinch of salt and pepper.

5 Remove the pork from the saucepan and thinly slice. Drain the cooking juices and reserve, discarding the other ingredients.

6 Cook the ramen in a large pan of boiling water according to the package directions. Drain under cold running water to rinse off the starch.

7 Heat the chicken stock, adding the 1/2 bouillon cube if a stronger soup is required. Stir until the cube dissolves.

8 Warm up the corn in boiling water and drain.

9 Put 2 tablespoons of the cooking juices put aside earlier into each of four individual noodle bowls. Add the hot stock to half-fill the bowls. Put a quarter each of the ramen, sliced pork, bean sprouts, spinach, and corn on top. Sprinkle with the chopped scallion and serve hot with rayu.

meat stock

Strainers and skimmers are vital for successful stockmaking. They remove fat, solid matter and impurities, resulting in a clear, sediment-free stock. For a brown stock, brown the bones first in a hot oven, pouring off any fat before adding them to the stockpot.

Makes about 2¹/₂ quarts

Tools	Ingredients
cook's knife	About 7¹/₂ lb. beef or veal bones
stockpot	
skimmer or perforated spoon	2 large onions, chopped
	2 large carrots, chopped
colander	2 celery sticks, chopped
large piece cheesecloth	7 oz. mushrooms, sliced
	1¹/₄ cups dry white wine
	1 bouquet garni, fresh or dried
	¹/₂ tsp. black peppercorns

1 Put all the ingredients in a stockpot. Add 11 quarts of cold water (a) and bring to a boil. Don't add salt at this stage—it's better to add it to the dish in which the stock will be used.

2 As the liquid reaches boiling point, a harmless scum forms. Scoop this off with a skimmer or perforated spoon and discard (b). Turn the heat to a simmer and continue to skim off the scum. Cook, uncovered, for up to an hour until the mixture has reduced by at least half.

3 Remove the pan from the heat and let the stock stand for 30 minutes. This allows debris to settle.

4 Line a colander with wet cheesecloth. Slowly pour the stock through the cloth, leaving the debris behind (c). For a clearer stock, pour the liquid through the cloth again. Cool the stock, then chill. Scrape off any fat that forms on the surface.

chicken stock

This gelatinous stock forms part of the "pumpkin and girolle soup" recipe contributed by Alain Ducasse (see page 60). The stock differs from others in that the chicken carcasses are brought to a boil quickly, then boiled for 5 minutes, during which time the scum is removed—most recipes specify that this stage is carried out slowly. After rapid boiling, the carcasses are drained and returned to the pan with fresh water, and the usual slow simmering begins. This method certainly speeds things up, and the finished stock is delicious.

Makes about 2¹/₂ quarts

Tools	Ingredients
cook's knife	About 7¹/₂ lb. raw chicken carcasses and/or parts
vegetable peeler	
stockpot	2 onions, quartered
skimmer or perforated spoon	1 large leek, green parts only, rinsed well and cut into 2-inch pieces
strainer or colander	1 carrot, halved
large piece cheesecloth	2 celery stalks, cut into 2-inch pieces
large bowl	1 tomato, quartered
	6 parsley stems
	1 tbsp. coarse sea salt
	1 tsp. black peppercorns

1 Place the chicken in a large stockpot. Cover with cold water and bring to a boil over high heat. Boil for 5 minutes, skimming the surface frequently.

2 Drain the chicken and rinse under cold water. Rinse out the stockpot to remove the scum, return the chicken to the pot, and cover with cold water.

3 Add the vegetables, parsley stems, salt, and peppercorns, and bring to a boil over high heat. Reduce the heat and cook, uncovered, at the barest simmer for 2 hours, without stirring or skimming. Remove from the heat and let cool briefly.

4 Strain the stock through a strainer or colander lined with cheesecloth, into a large bowl. Let the stock cool completely, then store covered in the refrigerator for no more than 24 hours, or freeze in small containers.

5 Before using, scrape off and discard the fat that forms on the surface.

boiling
and
steaming

basic saucepans

Along with knives, saucepans can be your pride and joy, for it is within them
that your efforts at chopping, slicing, mixing, measuring, and seasoning culminate,
and the alchemy that is cooking takes place. Because of this, saucepans are more
complex than knives. Knives are about cutting and the results are instant and
obvious. Saucepans require patience and cooperation. You have less control over
the way they behave, and for successful results, you must get to know how they
react with different ingredients and heat levels.

My earliest pots and pans were not of the best quality, being made of thin aluminum or coated
with quaintly speckled enamel. I did not treat them well, nor they me. However, though they warped
and buckled, burned me and the food, they did not succeed in dampening my embryonic passion
for cooking. Since then I have amassed a collection, and the more I cook, the better quality I buy.

There's no denying good pots and pans are expensive. As with knives, it's worth starting off with
three or four good ones that earn their keep, rather than buying several of inferior quality. There
is a growing number of so-called "chef's sets" on the market, but don't be tempted by them. You
will inevitably end up with pans you never use because you don't cook the type of food for which
they are intended. They also take up valuable storage space. You may of course be given a set of
pans, perhaps as a wedding present, but this leaves you the problem of having to live up to their
demands. If you are new to cooking, you may feel pressured into embarking on recipes that are
overambitious or simply not your style. It is far better to build up your collection of pans gradually
and let your culinary repertoire expand at its own pace.

1 Nonstick aluminum saucepan Sturdily built but not too heavy,
this pan is made from nonwarping cast aluminum, coated inside
and out with a SilverStone® nonstick surface. This makes for
fat-free cooking and easy cleaning, so it is a good pan for sauces,
porridge, scrambled eggs, and other foods that stick. Suitable for
all stovetops except the induction type, the pan has a thick
ground base for fast, even heat distribution. The ovenproof glass
lid has a heat-resistant knob. This pan is available in blue, green,
or black, and in three sizes, from 1 1/4 to 2 1/2 quarts.

2 Stainless-steel saucepans These sleek, professional pans are
made in top-grade 18/10 stainless steel (see "material choice,"
page 8). The base has an aluminum/magnetic steel/aluminum
core sealed between two layers of stainless steel. This means
the pans are suitable for all stovetops, including the induction
type, which is activated by magnetism. The handles are welded
to the body of the pan over a large area so they cannot come
loose. They are comfortable to hold but tend to get hot when
cooking at high temperatures. Despite this minor drawback,
these pans are a joy to use. They are available in five sizes, from
1 quart to 5 1/4 quarts, and it's worth having all five; otherwise,
aim for the largest, the smallest, and one in the middle.

Choosing saucepans Before buying, think carefully about how you will use and store your saucepans. Size, shape, weight, and material (see "material choice," page 8) are all-important.

A basic set of saucepans might consist of a couple of smallish pans, say 1 1/2 to 2 quarts, one or two medium pans (3 1/2 to 4 quarts), and a large pan (5 1/2 quarts). A very small pan (4 1/2 cups) is useful for melting butter, boiling eggs, or reheating small amounts of food, and a small nonstick milk pan is a must for heating milk.

The base should be thick and solid—a thin base will buckle over high heat, making it useless on a sealed cooking plate. The base of a good-quality pan is ground flat as opposed to stamped flat; check for the marks of the grinding machine. Test for flatness by placing the pan on a level surface and pressing to see if it wobbles.

If your stovetop has radiant rings, measure the rings and buy pans to fit. The perfect pan should fit exactly over the heating element. This keeps the heat where it is meant to be—under the pan.

A pouring lip will cope with a thin liquid like milk, but not a thick sauce or soup. If the pan is to be used by a left hander, you will need a left-handed pan or one with two pouring lips or a continuous pouring rim that lets you pour from any point. A pouring rim also pours large amounts of liquid and thick liquids more efficiently.

Handles should be long enough to distance your hand from the heat. They must be comfortable to hold and firmly attached to the pan. Rivets or a firm weld are better than screws. Pans that hold 3 1/4 quarts or more should have two handles—either a pair of ears, or one ear opposite a long handle. Handles and knobs of lids should be heat resistant. If metal, they should conduct heat less well than the pan. If your pan is intended to go in the oven, the knob and handle need to be heatproof. Lids are essential for steaming, poaching, and stewing, and for bringing water to a boil sooner. They should fit snugly, especially if you want to use the pan for steaming.

Material science The two basic properties required of a material used for pan making are that the surface is nonreactive so it will not taint the food's flavor, and that it conducts heat efficiently and evenly. As no single material meets these requirements, manufacturers use combinations of metals. For example, the base may be made from a layer of aluminum or copper (both chemically reactive, but excellent conductors of heat) sandwiched between stainless steel (a poor heat conductor, but nonreactive to chemicals). Another solution is to coat the inside of the pan, and sometimes the outside too, with a nonreactive substance such as vitreous enamel, or to treat it electrolytically by anodizing, as in anodized aluminum. Anodizing hardens aluminum and makes it nonreactive.

3 Anodized aluminum saucepans These hard-anodized pans are not cheap, but they are guaranteed for life. The base is heavy and solid, and the grey anodized coating will not chip, peel, or scratch when scrubbed.

The cast stainless-steel handles are triple riveted to the body and stay cool in use. The larger pans have a helper handle opposite the long one so you can lift it with both hands. They are available in four sizes, from 1 1/2 to 4 3/4 quarts.

4 Anodized aluminum milk pan As boiling milk tends to stick to the pan, this is one of the few saucepans that needs a nonstick surface. This one, in heavy-gauge aluminum, has an anodized surface on the exterior and a hard-wearing, easy-to-clean, nonstick interior. The stainless-steel handle is firmly riveted. If you are left handed, make sure your pan has a pouring lip on both sides.

beyond basics

As your cooking skills develop and you gain in confidence, you will undoubtedly start to yearn for more pots and pans. The ones shown here are the next step up from a basic set and will ease tasks such as preserving and making soups and sauces. Buy them according to need. Some of these pans are quite large, which

1 Stockpot with pasta insert If you care about good soup, a stockpot is almost a basic requirement. This large stainless-steel pot accommodates several pounds of meat, bone, and vegetables. The tall, somewhat narrow shape slows evaporation of liquid and allows solid matter to remain submerged for hours at a time, while coaxing out delicious flavors. A five-layer ground base (see 3 Double boiler) permits prolonged simmering without scorching. The generously sized and firmly welded U-shaped handles make for safe lifting.

The pasta insert lifts out easily, leaving the cooking water behind—a process that is easier and safer than carrying a heavy pot from stovetop to sink. Those who wear glasses will also appreciate steamfree lenses. The insert doubles up as a strainer when blanching vegetables.

2 Pressure cooker Pressure cookers work by trapping steam by means of an especially designed tight-fitting lid. As pressure builds up, the temperature rises above boiling point, and steam is forced into the food, reducing cooking time and cutting down on fuel.

This stainless-steel model has a domed lid housing a self-regulating valve, which limits the amount of escaping steam. Normal cooking time is reduced by at least one third. The solid ground base is suitable for all stovetops, including the induction type.

3 Double boiler This stainless-steel pan has a well-fitting lid and a solid, five-layer base—a core of silver alloy/copper/silver alloy is sandwiched between two layers of stainless steel, giving excellent heat conduction.

Simmering water in the lower pan gently heats the base of the upper one without touching it. This is an infallible way of making egg-based sauces such as hollandaise—the gentle heat keeps egg proteins from coagulating, as they do in scrambled eggs, so they are able to emulsify with butter to form a smooth and silky sauce.

Used either on its own or with the lid, the bottom part of this pan doubles as a saucepan or Dutch oven.

4 Copper saucepan A copper pan is the Rolls Royce of cookware. This splendid saucepan encapsulates the properties of three different metals: copper for speedy and even conduction of heat, a taint-free stainless-steel lining—far more durable than traditional tin—and a stay-cool, cast-iron handle. The only drawback is that once you have one copper pan, you'll want more.

might be off-putting if you have limited storage space. However, because they can perform two or three functions, they may actually help you to economize on space as well as money. For example, a large stockpot is well worth having as it can double up as a pasta pot and, even though it does not have the flaring sides that help evaporation, as a preserving pan. A pressure cooker without its lid makes a very useful large saucepan.

5 Preserving pan This capacious, 14 1/4-quart, stainless-steel cauldron will satisfy the needs of the most dedicated jam-maker. It has a solid ground, wide base to ensure even heat distribution, and gently flaring sides that increase the surface area and encourage evaporation. The invaluable helper handle assists with lifting and pouring, while the semicircular handle across the top can be locked in an upright position to keep the pan cooler.

6 Slant-sided aluminum saucepan Made from heavy-gauge aluminum with a 1/4-inch ground base, this simple pan is perfect for sauces. The narrow base speeds up boiling, and the splayed sides increase the surface area, encouraging evaporation and reduction of liquids. A continuous turned edge means you can pour from any position without messy drips. The bakelite handle remains cool during cooking. It is best not used for cooking vegetables as uncoated aluminum will cause them to discolor.

8 Bain marie Any saucepan can be turned into a double boiler with this "universal" stainless-steel bain marie. Place it in the top of the pan above simmering water and it will heat the contents gently and evenly. This is an ideal way of making egg-based sauces and custards, melting chocolate or cheese, or reheating leftovers without scorching them.

9 Butter melter This neat little stainless-steel pan, measuring just 4 1/2 inches in diameter, is designed for warming or clarifying small amounts of butter. It is attractive enough to be brought to the table, for example to pour butter over asparagus. You can also use it for warming brandy or melting chocolate. It has just one pouring lip, so left-handed users either have to pour "backwards" or use their right hand.

7 Slant-sided anodized aluminum saucepan
Altogether more sophisticated with its gray anodized coating and stainless-steel handle, this 1-quart pan is similar in design and use to the uncoated aluminum pan. Use it for reducing sauces, making gravy, or warming hot chocolate. Two pouring spouts make it suitable for left or right handers. It is also available in a 2 1/2-quart size, which makes a brilliant sauté pan. The larger size has a continuous turned rim instead of pouring lips, making it easier to pour out solids and liquids.

Blanching This is a method of partially cooking vegetables by immersing them briefly in rapidly boiling water. Vegetables that are to be frozen are blanched to halt enzyme activity. It is a method used by chefs to cook vegetables ahead of serving—they can be quickly reheated with no loss of flavor or texture. After blanching, vegetables are best plunged into a bowl of ice water, a process known as "refreshing." This also has the effect of heightening the color, especially in green vegetables.

Reducing You can make quick gravy to serve with pan-fried meats, such as chops or steak, cooked in a sauté pan. After cooking, remove the meat to a serving dish and keep warm. Add a small glass of wine to the pan juices and stir well, scraping up any meaty deposits with a wooden spoon. Boil rapidly to reduce by a third, then pour in 2 to 3 tablespoons of cream or crème fraîche. Allow the gravy to bubble for a few seconds, add seasoning, and pour over the meat.

Simmering Cooking a casserole or stew at a simmer, with the occasional bubble breaking the surface, helps soften the collagen in meat tissues, making tough meat more tender. Adding acidic ingredients, such as tomatoes and wine, also helps tenderize. A casserole dish with a heavy metal base allows for gentle simmering.

Gentle boiling The turbulent action of fast boiling can break up the texture of certain foods, such as floury potatoes, as the starch swells. When boiling point is reached, turn the heat to a gentle boil. Some starchy foods can boil over if the heat is too high—for example, pasta and rice. A tablespoon of oil helps to maintain surface tension.

specialized pans

These pans are marvelous to have for those times when you get the urge to whip up zabaglione or boil caramel, for example. Though they tend to be expensive, it is a pleasure to use pans in which form so closely follows function. The rounded shape of the zabaglione pan perfectly echoes the shape of the whisk used to create the foam. The fondue pot is wide and shallow enough for several people to dip their forks at once without being overcrowded. The flared sides of the polenta pan increase the surface area and encourage evaporation.

1 Polenta pan Known as a "paiolo" in Italy, this beautiful copper pan makes the rather arduous process of stirring polenta a pleasure rather than a chore. The pot heats quickly and evenly, while flared sides make prolonged stirring easier. The shapely wooden handle stays cool and comfortable during stirring. The pan is unlined and should therefore be rubbed with vinegar and salt before and after each use (see "Meringues," page 49).

2 Zabaglione pan This solid copper pan is designed to froth up the warm, creamy alcoholic custard known as "zabaglione" in Italy and "sabayon" in France. Set over a low flame or double boiler, the copper conducts even, gentle heat, which softly coagulates the egg proteins as you whisk. The deep, rounded bowl facilitates the rapid scooping movement needed to create the foam.

3 Sugar boiler This attractive copper pan is ingeniously designed to cope with the very high temperatures produced during sugar boiling. The pan is unlined because the traditional tin lining would melt (see "material choice," page 8), and sugar does not react adversely with copper. You might expect the handle to be made of wood, which remains cool, but at the temperatures reached wood might catch fire. Even oven mitts are in danger of igniting. The problem is solved by the hollow copper handle, into which chefs traditionally insert a length of broomstick. Because the handle is funnel shaped, the wood is in contact with only a small area of hot metal, so the wood does not catch fire and it prevents heat from being conducted to the end where your hand is.

4 Saucier Normally found only in the professional kitchen, this saucier is made from best-quality 18/10 stainless steel (see "material choice," page 8). It has an inner core of aluminum, not just in the base but all the way up the sides, for optimum heat conductivity. The pan can be used on all stovetops, including the magnetic induction type.

The rounded, slightly flared sides facilitate easy stirring and whisking, and restrict splattering. The pan is perfect for reducing liquids, as well as browning meat and sautéing vegetables. It comes in four sizes, from 1 to 5 1/2 quarts.

5 Cheese-fondue pot A traditional cheese fondue consists of cheese and wine melted together in a pot over a flame. Diners spear chunks of bread on forks and swirl them in the communal pot, which is known as a "caquelon" in France and Switzerland. As high temperatures make cooked cheese stringy, cheese-fondue pots are traditionally made of glazed earthenware, which withstand only gentle heat. Meat-fondue pots are made of metal. Popular in the seventies, and a ubiquitous item on the wedding-present list, fondue sets seem to be making a comeback.

basic polenta

Polenta is a mild-tasting grain with a deeply satisfying flavor. Cooked to a porridge-like consistency it can be served wet, like mashed potatoes, or cooled and cut into shapes, then broiled or fried until crisp—delicious for mopping up tasty juices and gravy.

Polenta is traditionally made in a special pan (see page 69), but a large, heavy-based saucepan makes a good substitute. The hot mixture will spurt upward as it cooks, so use a long-handled wooden spoon to avoid being scalded.

Tools

polenta pan or large, heavy-based saucepan
long-handled wooden spoon
wooden board or wide, shallow pan
flexible metal spatula

Ingredients

7 cups water
1 tsp. salt
2 1/2 cups polenta

1 Bring the water and salt to a boil in a polenta pan or large saucepan, then turn down to a medium simmer. Stirring with one hand, use the other to add the polenta in a steady stream, holding your fist in a funnel shape (a).

2 Continue to add the polenta, making sure each fistful is absorbed before adding another. Traditionally, polenta is stirred in one direction only (b).

3 Polenta is best stirred for up to 20 minutes. It is cooked when it comes away from the side of the pan (c).

4 To serve polenta wet, simply spoon it into a serving dish. Otherwise, pour it onto a board or a wide, shallow pan, level the top with a wet spatula, and allow to cool and firm before frying or grilling (d).

broiled polenta with mushrooms, celery root, and sage

This recipe uses polenta that is slightly stiffer than the basic mixture, and is particularly suitable for cutting into shapes before frying and broiling. Use two or three different kinds of cultivated or wild mushrooms such as chanterelles or oyster, shiitake, cremini, or portobello.

Serves 4 to 6 as an appetizer or light meal

Tools	Ingredients
polenta pan or large, heavy-based saucepan	2 1/4 cups water
long-handled wooden spoon	1/2 tsp. salt
7 1/2- x 7 1/2-inch roasting pan	3/4 cup polenta
flexible metal spatula	2 tbsp. olive oil, plus extra for brushing polenta
cook's knife	2 tbsp. butter
broiler pan	2 tbsp. chopped fresh sage
pastry brush	1 cup celery root, peeled and diced
vegetable peeler	18 oz. assorted mushrooms, cut into bite-size chunks if large
small skillet	
tongs	2 garlic cloves, finely chopped
large skillet	1 tbsp. chopped flat-leaf parsley
	squeeze of lemon juice
	pinch of cayenne pepper
	sea salt and freshly ground black pepper
	small sage sprigs, to garnish

1 Cook the polenta following steps 1 to 3 of "basic polenta" (see opposite). Pour the polenta into a small, square roasting pan and level the surface with a wet spatula. Leave to cool.

2 Heat the broiler to very hot. Meanwhile, slice the polenta into six rectangles, then halve each rectangle diagonally to make two triangles. Brush both sides with olive oil, and spread out in a broiler pan.

3 Heat 1 tablespoon each of the oil and butter in a small skillet. Add half the sage and gently fry for a few seconds to flavor the oil. Add the celery root and fry over medium heat for a few minutes, turning the celery with tongs until lightly colored on all sides. Remove the pan from the heat and set aside.

4 Heat another tablespoon of butter and oil in a large skillet. Fry the remaining sage for a few seconds, then throw in the mushrooms. Stir-fry over moderately high heat for 7 to 9 minutes until most, but not all, of the liquid has evaporated. Add a little more oil if necessary.

5 While the mushrooms are cooking, broil the polenta pieces until golden and crisp at the edges, then turn them over and broil the other side.

6 Keeping an eye on the polenta, tip the contents of the celery-root pan into the mushrooms, and add the garlic. Fry for another minute, then add the parsley, lemon juice, and seasonings.

7 Divide the polenta triangles between individual plates and pile the mushroom mixture on top. Garnish with the sage sprigs.

coffee...

Coffee-making at its most basic is simply a matter of pouring boiling or near-boiling water over fresh grounds and allowing them to steep. However, during nine centuries of coffee-drinking, brewing equipment has proliferated. Despite the many options, there is no best way to brew coffee, though aficionados will swear by a particular method. Whether you like to kick-start the day with a blast of espresso or prefer something mild, the best way is how you like to make it.

1 Drip-filter coffeemaker This electric coffeemaker has a convenient swing-out filter holder operated by a press button, a front-filling water tank, and a magnified water-level indicator.

To use a drip-filter machine, fill the cone-shaped filter with finely ground coffee, and then with boiling water, which filters through into the carafe. The cone shape permits fast saturation of the grounds, while the density of the filter slows down the rate at which water passes through. The filter also absorbs some of the coffee's natural oils, resulting in a brew that is light and clear but somewhat lacking in body.

2 Percolator Something of a museum piece, this device forces boiling water up through a hollow central shaft and showers it over the coffee grounds suspended at the top of the shaft in a perforated container. The water drips back to the bottom of the pot, via the container, and thus continually boils and circulates until the indicator light shows the coffee is ready. The device produces a somewhat "stewed" brew that nevertheless has its fans.

Espresso makers
4 This traditional aluminum machine can be used on the stove top. Fill the bottom container with water, insert a funnel-shaped filter and fill it with medium-ground coffee. Then screw the top section to the lower. Once heated, water and steam are forced through the grounds and on through a narrow shaft in the top container. A high-octane brew then gushes out of the top of the shaft, filling the upper container. It is available in 3-, 6-, 9-, and 12-cup sizes.
5 The "designer" espresso maker works in a similar way, except the coffee shoots into the cup through a down-turned shaft. It comes in 1- and 2-cup sizes.

6 Plunger coffeemaker This is one of the simplest ways to make a rich brew. Pour boiling water over coarsely ground coffee in the base of the glass beaker. After five minutes of steeping, press the plunger—two filter disks attached to a central shaft—down over the grounds. This traps them in the base of the beaker and leaves the coffee ready to pour. When buying, make sure the disks fit tightly into the beaker, or grounds will escape up the side. One drawback is that the coffee does not maintain its temperature while steeping. This can be overcome by using an insulated cover; newer models have an acrylic outer casing, which retains heat better.

3 Cappuccino frother To create the essential froth for your cappuccino, fill the container halfway with milk, heat until it is almost boiling, then put on the lid and pump the plunger for about 30 seconds. Alternatively, you can heat the milk in a saucepan and froth it with a spiral whisk.

... and tea

Like coffee, properly made tea needs clean-tasting, freshly drawn and boiled water. A kettle is essential—even though water boils equally well in a saucepan, it is simply not the same. Water is more easily poured from a kettle's spout, and because the water is enclosed, it boils more quickly and uses less fuel.

There was a time when a kettle was simply a kettle; nowadays there are numerous designs. If you are choosing a kettle to use on the stovetop, look for one with a broad, flat base to maximize contact with the heat source and speed up boiling. The handle should be positioned well above the lid, and the spout should direct steam away from your hand. If you want an electric kettle, bear in mind that the tall jug type needs less water to cover the heating element, so it boils water more quickly and uses less electricity than the traditionally shaped sort. Some are fitted with a fine mesh filter just behind the spout to separate out the sediment that may accumulate in hard-water areas.

There is no doubt that tea is better made from loose leaves that are allowed a five-minute steep in a teapot, rather than from a teabag pressed hurriedly into a cup. Like kettles, teapots come in a range of styles, materials, colors, and shapes. Tea seems to taste better when made in a glazed china or earthenware pot. Glass and stainless-steel pots also work well but are more expensive.

Whatever the material, there are three main features to look for: a non-drip spout, a lid that stays in place as you pour the last cup, and a handle large enough to distance your knuckles from the pot.

1 Whistling kettle The Alessi Kettle with Bird, designed in 1985, has become something of a modern design icon. It fulfils all the essential requirements of a stovetop kettle, possessing a wide, thick base, a comfortable, heatproof handle that positions your hand away from the steam, and a cheerful whistle.

2 Cordless electric kettle Clean and almost surgical in appearance, this electric kettle has no trailing electrical cord and is good-looking enough to be used in the most stylish surroundings. A see-through indicator enables you to measure the amount of water and prevents over-filling.

3 Traditional kettle This simple kettle is made in enameled steel and comes in a range of bright colors, as well as black or white. The handle and the knob on the lid are heat resistant. The solid ground base is suitable for all types of stovetops, including the induction type and the solid heating plates of range cookers.

4 China teapot
This classic white porcelain teapot has a pleasingly fat spout, a round knob for lifting the lid, and a capacious, curved handle. An integral filter prevents stray tea leaves from escaping into your cup.

5 Glass teapot/ tea press This elegant teapot works in the same way as a plunger coffeemaker. Tea leaves are held in a perforated container while steeping. When the tea looks the right color, press down the plunger and remove the central insert.

poachers and steamers

Poaching and steaming are beautifully simple methods of allowing clean, natural flavors to shine through. In fact, steamed food can make a welcome change from a surfeit of chargrilling, searing, and stir-frying. If you're on a low-fat diet, steamed food is definitely worth trying, and if you cook in cramped conditions or are without an oven, steaming food in tiered containers can be a lifesaver, as the Chinese have known for centuries.

Poaching is a technique that falls midway between boiling and steaming. Foods such as chicken or fish are laid on a rack in a pan with just enough liquid to cover the bottom, and simmered very gently until they are barely cooked. The food remains wonderfully moist and, because it has not been subjected to vigorous boiling, keeps its shape.

As the name suggests, steaming is a method of cooking food in the vapors that rise from boiling cooking liquid, which may be water, stock, or wine. Virtually any food can be steamed: meat, poultry, seafood, or vegetables. It is mainly the Asian cuisines—Thai, Japanese, and Chinese—that make the most of the techique. Food is placed on a plate or in a perforated container set above the liquid and covered with a lid to keep the steam in. Because the food is not in direct contact with the liquid, fewer nutrients are lost by leaching. If the liquid is water, it will be nicely flavored by the food being steamed, and can be used to make a gravy or sauce, or for cooking rice.

If you have never tried steaming, start off with a "universal" steamer insert, or a fold-out steamer. Then you can progress to a more expensive multitiered set. Some items, such as fish kettles or asparagus steamers, are expensive and worth buying only if you are likely to use them regularly. On the other hand, a plum-pudding steamer costs little and is fun to have even if you use it only once a year.

2 Three-piece steamer You can cook a complete meal with this 8-inch diameter, tiered steamer set. Made of top-quality 18/10 stainless steel, the bottom pan has a thick ground base for maximum heat conduction and for use on any stovetop, including the induction type. The bottom pan can be used to simmer a stew, while large vegetables such as cauliflower steam in the deep middle container, and smaller vegetables steam in the top. The lid fits all three parts so you can use the base alone or with one steamer basket only.

1 Couscousier This two-tiered aluminum pot is designed for cooking the North African semolina-based dish couscous. The lower pot stews meat, poultry, or vegetables in a fragrant broth, from which steam rises through the upper pot's perforated base to cook the couscous above.

3 Bamboo steamers Pleasing and inexpensive, these Chinese steamers can be used for a variety of foods, such as whole fish, pieces of poultry, vegetables, or dumplings. They come in various sizes and can be stacked as high as you like in a wok or pan of boiling water. New steamers should be soaked for 15 minutes to get rid of the pervasive smell of bamboo.

4 Rice ball Save on cleaning the pan and cook rice in a perforated rice steamer. The perforations are small enough to prevent uncooked grains of rice escaping. It is important not to overfill the steamer as rice doubles in volume once cooked. The chain has a hook on the end so you can hang it from the side of the pan.

5 Steaming trivet This classic design has not changed much since its inception. The trivet sits in the bottom of a pan of simmering water and raises a smaller pan or bowl off the surface, creating a makeshift bain marie. The grooved surface helps to prevent pans from slipping off the stand. It can also be used as a trivet to protect the countertop from hot pans.

6 Plum-pudding steamer This solid steamer is perfect for making a traditional round plum pudding. A cluster of perforations at the top lets the steam escape. Suspend the steamer from the handle of a wooden spoon resting on opposite sides of the pan.

7 Expandable steamer basket Suitable for most saucepans, this compact stainless-steel steamer opens out like the petals of a flower. The perforations and gaps between the overlapping petals allow steam to penetrate well and the feet raise the food above the boiling water. The central stalk limits the ways in which you can arrange the food, but on some models the stalk is removable. The steamer is available in two sizes, expanding from 5 1/2 to 9 inches, and from 7 to 11 inches.

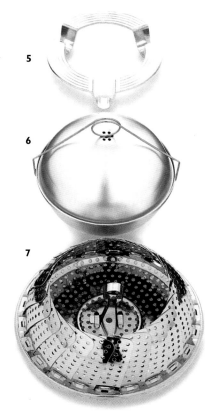

8 Asparagus steamer Some cooks think that if asparagus stalks are cooked until tender, the tips will be overcooked. This tall, narrow steamer allows the stalks to stand upright in boiling water while the tips cook in the steam. However, if you don't mind stalks a little on the crunchy side, you could just lay the spears flat in an ordinary steamer.

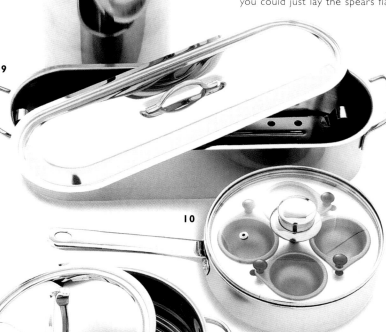

9 Fish kettle/poacher Small or medium-sized fish can be poached in any pan into which a rack will fit, but large, round fish such as salmon need an elongated pan that allows the fish to lie flat. The fish is placed on a perforated, two-handled rack that lifts easily from the pan, draining the fish without spoiling its shape. Some fish kettles are so large they will straddle two burners. There is also a glamorous diamond-shaped kettle designed especially for poaching flat fish such as halibut and turbot.

10 Egg poacher Though it is not a poacher in the strict sense, as the eggs are cooked by steam, this magnificent pan not only cooks flawless eggs but, without the insert, doubles up as a nonstick sauté pan. Made in top-quality 18/10 stainless steel (see "material choice," page 8), the poacher has nonstick, removable egg cups, and a 1/4-inch thick, encapsulated base suitable for all types of stovetops.

11 "Universal" steamer insert Sit the stepped base of this perforated container in any of your saucepans, and you have an instant steamer for cooking vegetables, fish, meat, or poultry. It is an indispensable utensil.

tunisian couscous with greens, bell peppers, and garlic

The recipe for this traditional Tunisian dish was contributed by Paula Wolfert, the award-winning food writer whose speciality is Mediterranean and Middle Eastern cuisine. The melange of dill, fennel and celery leaves, red-pepper flakes, and spices makes for a light and delicious couscous, which Paula suggests serving with glasses of buttermilk, as is the custom. If you don't have an authentic North African couscousier (see page 74), use a large saucepan with a tightly fitting steamer insert. If fennel leaves are hard to find, increase the amount of dill. Tabil is a Tunisian spice paste, which you can buy from shops specializing in Middle Eastern Food.

Serves 6

Tools

cook's knife or mezzaluna

garlic press

paring knife

couscousier or large saucepan with steamer insert

large skillet

wooden spoon or turner

long fork

tongs

Ingredients

1/2 cup chopped dill leaves

1/2 cup chopped fennel leaves

1/2 cup chopped flat-leaf parsley

handful of celery leaves, chopped

handful of carrot tops, chopped

1 large scallion, thinly sliced

1/2 small leek, thinly sliced

1/2 cup olive oil

1 small onion, chopped

3 tbsp. tomato paste

5 large garlic cloves, crushed

2 tsp. sweet paprika

2 tsp. salt, or more, to taste

2 tsp. ground coriander or tabil

1 tsp. ground caraway

1 1/2 to 2 tsp. dried red-pepper flakes, preferably Aleppo, Turkish, or Near East pepper for best flavor

2 cups water

2 1/2 cups medium-grain couscous

1 fresh green chili, stemmed, seeded, and finely chopped

1 red bell pepper, stemmed, seeded, and cut into 6 pieces

6 garlic cloves, peeled and left whole

1 Fill the bottom of the couscousier or saucepan with water and bring to a boil. Put the perforated top or steamer insert in place. Add all the green leaves, scallions, and leeks. Cover and steam for 30 minutes (a).

2 Remove from the heat and allow to cool, uncovered. When cool enough to handle, squeeze out the excess moisture and set aside.

3 Heat the oil in a large skillet and add the onion. Gently fry for 2 to 3 minutes to soften, then add the tomato paste. Cook, stirring, until the paste glistens.

4 Add the crushed garlic, paprika, salt, coriander or tabil, caraway, and red-pepper flakes. Cook slowly until the mixture is well blended. Add 1 cup water, cover, and cook for 15 minutes.

5 Remove the pan from the heat. Stir the dry couscous into the contents of the pan and stir until well blended (b). Stir in the steamed greens, leeks, and scallions, and mix well. Fold in the green chili, pieces of red pepper, and garlic cloves.

6 Add more water to the bottom of the couscousier or saucepan and bring to a boil. Put the top or steamer insert in place. Add the contents of the pan and steam, covered, for 30 minutes (c).

7 Turn out the couscous onto a large, warm, serving dish. Use a long fork to break up any lumps. Use tongs to fish out the whole garlic cloves and pieces of red pepper, putting them aside.

8 Stir 1 cup water into the couscous, check seasoning, and cover with foil. Set in a low oven for 10 minutes before serving.

9 When ready to serve, decorate the couscous with the slices of red pepper and whole garlic cloves. Serve with glasses of buttermilk.

steamed salmon with ginger, scallions, and bok choy

Steamed on a trivet over a wok, this comforting and easily digested dish is ideal if you are under stress or entertaining in a hurry. It needs nothing more than a simple accompaniment of plainly boiled white rice. Make sure the fish is very fresh.

Serves 4

Tools

paring knife
9-inch heatproof plate
steaming trivet
aluminum foil
wok with lid
another wok or
large, heavy-based
skillet
fish turner
small saucepan

Ingredients

4 salmon steaks or cutlets, each about 1-inch thick

2 tsp. finely chopped fresh gingerroot

2 tbsp. rice wine or dry sherry

1 tbsp. soy sauce

1/2 tsp. salt

4 tbsp. peanut oil

2 large scallions, green parts included, shredded, but with green and white parts kept separate

3 heads bok choy, quartered lengthways

good squeeze of lime juice

coarsely ground black pepper

2 tsp. sesame oil

1 Rinse the fish steaks, pat dry with paper towels and place in a single layer on a heatproof plate.

2 Combine the gingerroot, rice wine or dry sherry, soy sauce, and salt. Sprinkle this over the fish, rub it into the flesh, and leave for 20 minutes, turning once.

3 Place a steaming trivet in a wok and add enough water to reach halfway up the trivet. Bring to a boil, place the plate of fish on the trivet, and cover with a loose tent of foil. Adjust the heat so the water is just boiling and put the lid on the wok. Steam for 10 to 15 minutes until the fish is opaque and starting to flake.

4 While the fish is steaming, heat 2 tablespoons of peanut oil in a second wok or large, heavy-based skillet. When the oil is almost smoking, fry the white part of the scallions for 30 seconds. Throw in the bok choy and stir-fry for 4 to 5 minutes until the stems are just tender, but still crunchy. Splash with a good squeeze of lime. Arrange in small mounds on four warm serving plates.

Steaming in a wok You will need a metal or wooden steaming trivet (see page 75) and a domed lid, often sold with a wok set. Food is steamed on a heatproof plate set on the trivet in the base of the wok. If you like, you can wrap food such as small chicken breasts or fish steaks in waxed paper, as shown. Alternatively, bamboo steamers (see page 74) can be stacked on the trivet; they can also be used on a trivet in an ordinary saucepan.

5 Using a fish turner, carefully lift the fish pieces from the wok and place on top of the bok choy. Arrange the green scallions on top and sprinkle with several grindings of black pepper.

6 Heat the sesame oil and remaining 2 tablespoons of peanut oil in a small saucepan. When it is very hot, pour over the green scallions and fish. Serve immediately.

frying grilling and broiling

skillets

Using a skillet of the right shape, size, and material makes a marked difference to the cooking process and your finished dish. There is an enormous choice and a good pan is not cheap, so before buying think carefully about the type of food you cook and the type of stovetop you cook on.

Different-shaped pans suit different tasks: high-sided pans help prevent splattering; rounded, outward-sloping sides comfortably accommodate spoons and spatulas, making stirring easier; shallow sides help you to deftly slide the contents out of the pan. Size is equally important. Small amounts of food cooked in too large a pan will dry and burn; juices will spread too thinly and evaporate. On the other hand, if you crowd food into a pan, it will steam and stew instead of browning and crisping.

1 Round skillet The outwardly sloping sides allow you to slide a spatula in and out of the skillet with ease, while a wide diameter provides generous food-to-heat contact. It is made of warp-free cast aluminum with a superior Silverstone® nonstick coating and stainless-steel handle.

2 Wok Designed for continuous movement over high heat, the wok's conical shape tips food continually back to the center, where the heat is at its most intense. Because the food is constantly on the move during stir-frying, much less oil is needed, making it a healthy option. Round-bottomed woks are suitable for gas stovetops; a slightly flattened bottom works better on ceramic or electric stovetops. This one has wooden handles, which remain cool despite the intense heat generated from the wok.

3 Ridged, square skillet Falling midway between a skillet and a stovetop grill, this pan has a ridged base that lifts food clear of fat and gives appetizing stripes to steaks and chops. From the same maker as the round pan (1), it is made of cast aluminum with a durable nonstick coating.

4 Stainless-steel sauté pan Made from superior 18/10 stainless steel (see "material choice," page 8), this pan has a thick ground base for maximum heat contact. A wide diameter and high, straight sides allow quick, light frying of chicken quarters or large amounts of potatoes in relatively little fat. The high sides also prevent spattering or spilling as food is turned and shaken. Once the food is evenly browned, the pan can be partly or fully covered, enabling the contents to cook at a more gentle pace.

Which metal? To fry food, it must be heated quickly and evenly, so the best pans are made of heavy-gauge metals that are efficient conductors of heat (see "material choice," page 8). Copper pans lined with tin or stainless steel are superb, but they are also very expensive. Anodized cast aluminum is one of the best materials as long as it is medium to heavy gauge; lightweight pans tend to buckle and develop hot spots. Stainless steel looks stunning and is easy to clean, but used alone, does not conduct heat well. Combined with a thick layer of copper or aluminum, however, it is hard to beat.

Cast iron is heavy and initially slow to heat, but once hot it maintains its temperature and conducts heat evenly. A small cast-iron skillet is handy for dry-frying whole spices, but before buying a larger one, check that you can manage the weight, especially if you have weak wrists.

Heavy-gauge, untreated, mild steel is another option. It needs seasoning with oil and in time it builds up a heavy patina that makes the surface nonstick. Until then it needs careful treatment to prevent rusting. Untreated steel pans should never be washed, but simply wiped clean and oiled.

Nonstick pans have improved greatly in recent years, and are worth having not only because they are easy to clean, but also because there is something delectable about the way morsels of food slide around the pan, sizzling in their own tasty juices, rather than a bath of oil. A nonstick skillet not only enables you to cut down on fat, but also allows you to really taste the food.

Choosing skillets For a basic set, choose two or three round, heavy-based skillets for general use: one with a 10- to 11 1/4-inch diameter base, another with an 8-to 9-inch base. and possibly a third with a 7 1/4-inch base—invaluable for a solitary meal. You might also consider buying a large, high-sided sauté pan with a lid for poultry quarters or chunky potatoes. A small, sloping-sided pan is essential for omeletes or crêpes. If you like stir-fries, you will also need a wok, though a heavy-based skillet makes a reasonable alternative.

When buying a new pan, check the handle is firmly welded or riveted. If the pan is very big, an ear-shaped helper handle opposite the long one makes lifting safer. Some handles are cast in one piece with the pan. Though less likely to work loose, integral handles tend to become hotter than handles that are attached separately.

5 Splatter screen Frying causes splattering and spitting of fat, especially if moist food is added to hot oil (always pat food dry before frying). When placed over the pan, this fine-meshed screen keeps fat where it belongs.

6 Hard-anodized aluminum stir-fry pan Invaluable for a solo stir-fry, this 8-inch pan has a unique, long-lasting, nonstick surface that is covered with minute ridges. The flat bottom is suitable for all stovetops.

7 Steel omelete pan Smooth sloping sides and a flat bottom ease the deft maneuvers necessary for making a perfect omelete. Made from untreated steel (see "Which metal?," above), this pan deserves respect—use it only for frying omeletes or crêpes and treat it with care.

8 Hard-anodized aluminum chef's pan This invaluable pan can be used as a wok or, with its heat-toughened glass lid, as a Dutch oven. It has a heavy ground base for maximum heat conduction, a durable nonstick interior, and two stainless-steel handles for easy lifting.

beyond basics

These pans are tailor-made for a particular use. Some are expensive, and they all take up valuable storage space. Consider them only if you regularly cook, or plan to cook, the food for which they are intended. On the other hand, if you were to buy an oval fish fryer, you might eat fish more often, which is no bad thing; and the chestnut pan would be lovely to have at Christmas....

1 Crêpe pan Made of heavy-gauge aluminum with a durable Silverstone® nonstick surface, this pan will have you tossing crêpes like a pro. The smooth, 10-inch base allows batter to spread evenly and thinly as you rotate the pan, and the shallow sides facilitate flipping.

2 Oval pan This excellent heavy-gauge pan is just right for frying two or three plump fish to crisp perfection. The nonstick surface allows minimal fat to be used and prevents fish skins sticking to the pan. It can be cleaned in seconds.

3 Fajita pan This oval pan is designed for sizzling the cut of beef (skirt steak, resembling a "fajo" or belt) after which the dish was named. Made from hard-anodized aluminum, the pan rapidly reaches the high temperature needed. Widely flaring, shallow sides permit quick and easy turning and serving.

4 Blini pan From the same manufacturer as the crêpe pan, this neat 4³/₄-inch pan has smooth, rounded sides that encourage yeast-leavened batter to rise. The handle is long enough to distance your hand from the heat.

5 Danish cake pan With its seven rounded depressions, this hefty lump of cast iron cooks to perfection Danish "aebleskiver" (apple dumplings). Cast iron conducts and maintains the level of heat necessary for cooking the dumplings right to the center.

6 Karhai (Indian wok) As versatile as a Chinese wok, the karhai is used for frying or, with its lid in place, for slowly simmering meat, poultry, seafood, and legume dishes. Made of heavy-gauge carbon steel with a Xylan® nonstick surface, the karhai has up-tilting handles that enable you to carry it to the table.

8 Chestnut pan More of a roaster than a fryer, this broad, shallow pan is designed for toasting chestnuts over a gas flame or open fire. The wide perforations allow the skins to remain in contact with the flames and char, while the nut meat inside remains succulent. There is no better way to pass a winter evening.

7 Paella pan This capacious pan is designed to accommodate the wealth of ingredients that go into a paella. Made of fast-heating, hard-anodized aluminum, the pan has rounded, flaring sides for easy sautéing of chicken, chorizo, and seafood, and for stirring in rice. The thick ground base and ridged, nonstick surface prevents burning and sticking, while the magnificent domed stainless steel lid encourages steam to condense and keep the food moist. The pan has the customary two handles (instead of one long one) with which it can be carried safely to the table.

scallop and shiitake stir-fry

Contributed by Raymond Blanc, acknowledged as one of the world's finest chefs, this recipe reflects his insistence on fresh, top-quality produce and light, unmasked flavors. The stir-fry is a wonderful mixture of sweet and bitter, soft and crunchy. It is cooked in a nonstick chef's pan (see page 81), which, as Raymond says, "epitomizes where we are in our cooking today. It has a good design, weight, and excellent heat conduction. It's the best nonstick pan I've ever used; I adore the glass lid as I like to see what's going on inside the pan."

Serves 4 as an appetizer or light meal

Tools	Ingredients
preparation bowls	12 large scallops and their corals
cook's knife	2 tbsp. sesame oil
paring knife	3 tbsp. peanut oil
citrus juicer	7 oz. small shiitake mushrooms
large nonstick chef's pan or wok	2 heads baby bok choy, leaves left whole, stems sliced
long-handled wooden spoon or wok ladle	into 3/4-inch pieces
	1 cup sugar snap peas, sliced in half lengthways
	1 1/4-inch piece fresh gingerroot, finely chopped
	2 garlic cloves, finely chopped
	juice of 1 unsprayed lime
	salt and freshly ground black pepper

1 Cut each scallop in half and each coral into three pieces.

2 Heat a high-sided pan or wok with the two oils, add the scallops and corals, and toss for a minute over your highest heat.

3 Add the mushrooms, sliced bok choy stems, and sugar snap peas, then stir-fry for a further minute.

4 Spoon in the ginger and garlic, along with the bok choy leaves and a little water, and stir-fry all together for another minute or two until the leaves have wilted.

5 Add the lime juice, season to taste, then serve on four large, warm plates.

Variations Monkfish makes a wonderful substitute for the scallops, and if you can't find bok choy, use Chinese cabbage, choi-sum, or spinach. If you do not like shiitake mushrooms, any mushroom can be used instead.

chicken in a red-pepper sauce

The recipe for this colorful chicken dish was contributed by Madhur Jaffrey, best-selling author and authority on Indian food. The dish is cooked from start to finish in a karhai (see page 83), a versatile pan similar to a Chinese wok, and perfect for stir-frying, deep-frying, and leisurely braising.

Serves 4

Tools	Ingredients
cook's knife	1/2 large onion, coarsely chopped
paring knife	1-inch cube fresh gingerroot, coarsely chopped
blender or food processor	3 garlic cloves
rubber or plastic spatula	1/4 cup blanched, flaked almonds
karhai or wok with a lid	2 red bell peppers, deseeded and coarsely chopped
citrus juicer	1 tbsp. ground cumin
	2 tsp. ground coriander
	1/2 tsp. ground turmeric
	1/8 to 1/2 tsp. cayenne pepper
	2 tsp. salt
	7 tbsp. vegetable oil, such as sunflower
	21/4 lb. chicken pieces, skinned and cut into small serving pieces
	2/3 to 1 cup water
	2 tbsp. lemon juice
	1/2 tsp. coarsely ground black pepper
	cilantro leaves, to garnish

1 Combine the onion, ginger, garlic, almonds, bell peppers, cumin, coriander, turmeric, cayenne pepper, and salt in the container of a food processor or blender. Blend, pushing down with a spatula whenever you need to, until you have a paste.

2 Put the oil in a karhai or wok, preferably nonstick, and set it over medium-high heat. When hot, pour in all the paste. Stir and fry it for 10 to 12 minutes or until you can see the oil forming tiny bubbles around it.

3 Add the chicken with 1/3 cup water, the lemon juice, and the black pepper. Stir to mix in and bring to a boil. Cover, turn the heat to low, and simmer gently for 25 minutes, stirring occasionally, until the chicken is tender. Add a little more water if necessary.

4 Serve straight from the karhai or transfer to a serving dish. Garnish with cilantro leaves before serving.

total immersion

The equipment featured here is designed for deep-frying food in boiling fat. An enormous variety of foods, both sweet and savory, is cooked this way— batter-coated fish, french fries, fritters, meatballs, Spanish churros, Middle Eastern falafel and kibbeh, Asian rice balls and crispy noodles, Indian pakoras and confectionery, to name more than a few.

Because so many different foods can be deep fried, it is important that the cooking vessel does not absorb odors and is reasonably easy to clean. And as success depends on frying at the correct temperature, the material from which the pan is made must be able to conduct heat evenly and maintain its temperature. Most important of all, because a large quantity of boiling fat is an obvious hazard, the equipment must be safe to use.

1 Tempura pan This beautiful, heavy, iron pan is the secret to making faultlessly crisp tempura and other deep-fried foods. It transfers heat quickly and evenly, and keeps the oil at a stable 340°F to 360°F. The pan has a spout for pouring off oil, and a rack for draining and keeping morsels of food warm. It comes with a pair of chopsticks for cooking.

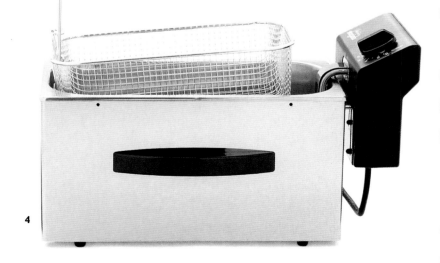

2 Deep-frying pan Made from high-quality enameled steel, this pan will not absorb smells or grease, and is easy to clean. It conducts heat well, and can be used on any stovetop, including the induction type. Fat drains easily from the inner wire basket, the handles of which have extensions that rest on the outer handles and lift the food clear of the fat below. The pan can also be used for blanching vegetables.

3 Potato nest fryers Finely shredded potatoes or other starchy foods are fried in the outer basket, while the smaller basket presses the contents into a nest shape. The inner basket is hinged to the outer one at the bowl end, and the two are held in place by a ring that fits over both handles. The handles are long enough to protect your hand from the heat of the fat.

4 Electric deep fryer This sensibly shaped deep fryer makes efficient use of storage space and allows you to deep-fry a whole fish without bending it. Like all electric fryers, this one is thermostatically controlled, but unlike most others, it filters cooking scraps into a cold zone between the heating element and the bottom of the pan. This ensures the oil stays clean and fresh for longer. With the exception of the heating element, all components can be put in a dishwasher. The fryer is supplied with a lid.

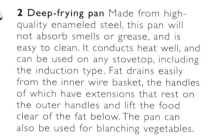

Deep-frying Successful deep-frying depends on so many variables that it could be called an art rather than a technique. The type, condition, and temperature of the oil, type and size of pan, the moisture content of the food, its porosity and surface area, the cooking time—all of these affect the quality of the finished product.

The type of fat or oil is critical. All fats and oils decompose once they reach a certain temperature—some may even spontaneously ignite. Once you can see and smell smoky fumes, or the fat becomes darker or flecked with particles, decomposition is under way. The point at which this happens is called "the smoke point." Butter and all animal fats have a low smoke point (about 375°F), which is why they quickly burn when overheated. Vegetable oils have a higher smoke point (about 450°F); peanut oil has one of the highest, which makes it the most suitable oil for deep-frying and stir-frying.

If you don't have a thermometer, you can check the temperature of the oil by dropping a small cube of bread into it. When the bread browns in 1 minute, the oil is ready to use.

The issue of whether oil can be reused is a contentious one. Although some cooks condone it, I would never do so, as successful deep-frying depends on getting the oil good and hot. Once oil has been heated to a high temperature, decomposition takes place rapidly and the flavor becomes tainted. If you do reuse oil, make sure you don't overheat it and that it is thoroughly strained after use.

French fries
1 After cutting, soak the raw fries in cold water for 30 minutes to remove excess starch. Drain and pat dry. Fill the fryer about a third full of peanut or sunflower oil. Heat the oil to 325°F. Place a large handful of raw fries in a wire basket and cook for 5 minutes, until pale golden.
2 Drain and increase the oil temperature to 375°F. Refry the fries for about a minute, until golden and crisp. Drain well and season.

Churros
3 Traditional Spanish churros are made with a choux pastry dough piped directly into hot peanut or sunflower oil using a ¹/₂-inch fluted tube. Fry at 350°F for 2 to 3 minutes until golden brown and crisp. Toss in superfine sugar and serve. Great served at breakfast, dipped into hot chocolate or coffee.

Tempura
4 To make Japanese tempura, dip thinly sliced vegetables or large peeled prawns into a lightly mixed batter of 2 egg yolks, 1¹/₄ cups of water, and 1¹/₃ cups of all-purpose flour. Deep-fry two or three pieces at a time in peanut or sunflower oil at 350°F, in a tempura pan or wok. Remove the cooked tempura and place them on the special rack to drain.

The direct heat of the broiler quickly seals succulent juices beneath a crisp exterior, and creates unique, intense flavors.

fired up

The choice of barbecue equipment grows each year. Before buying, it is vital to do some research and to consider the practicalities. As well as space, location, and storage issues, think about how many people you are likely to cook for. If a barbecue is too small the grill will become congested and food won't cook properly; if it's too big, you will waste fuel. For four to six people you need a grilling area at least 12 x 12 inches, or 14 inches in diameter.

Charcoal is by far the best fuel. Though they are convenient to use, gas and electric barbecues do not impart the same flavor. In any case, lighting, fanning, watching, and waiting are essential parts of the ritual. Choose irregularly shaped lumpwood charcoal rather than briquettes. It ignites easily, burns at a fierce heat and gives off a pleasing aroma. Scattering rosemary twigs on the coals once the food is cooking adds to the fragrance. Avoid instant-lighting charcoal or lighting agents unless you want the food to taste of gasoline.

All charcoal barbecues are made up of two components: a firebox that holds fuel and a rack that holds food. Many models include a grate to allow air to circulate under the fuel, and some have vents for regulating heat. Rack height is usually adjustable for controlling the cooking.

1 Long-handled utensils Tools with extra-long handles allow you to baste, spear, and turn while distancing your hands from the heat. The tongs are well sprung and have a ridged surface for efficient gripping. The slotted turner has a cleverly angled edge to prevent food from accidentally slipping off it. The brush allows you to safely anoint food with oil or a marinade without fear of drips and flare-up.

4 Disposable barbecue
Hardly atmospheric but great for a spur-of-the-moment picnic, disposable barbecues are usually ready to use in 15 to 20 minutes, and will often keep going for up to two hours. They are good for a couple of steaks or chops, or several sausages.

2 Oval portable barbecue
This rugged cast-iron barbecue is well suited to outdoor cooking. The rack can be set at two levels and is sturdy enough to support a pan, so can be used for boiling and simmering as well as grilling. A damper regulates heat and the flip-down lid allows you to add more fuel.

5 Wire holders
Turning whole items of food is made easier with these specially shaped wire holders. Brush with oil first to prevent sticking.

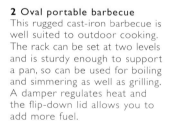

3 Hibachi barbecue Originally from Japan, these neat cast-iron barbecues are weighty but still portable. They have short legs and can be set on the ground if you don't mind squatting, or placed at table height on a fireproof surface. The fuel sits in a trough close to the rack, the height of which is adjustable. Though convenient and easy to use, hibachis have a small firebed so the fire doesn't last long. They are best used for small pieces of quick-cooking food.

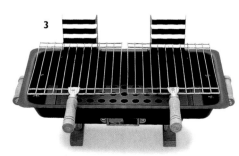

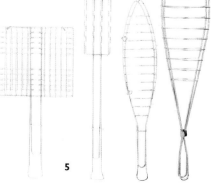

Choosing a barbecue

Barbecuing at its most basic requires no more than a cake rack set on two bricks. For many years this is what I used, and all I could afford; the results were delectable, or so they seemed at the time. Equally simple, but tidier, is a disposable barbecue, which consists of a heavy foil tray, firelighter, fuel, and a rack. All you need is a match.

Cast-iron portable barbecues, such as the hibachi, are hard-wearing and easy to use. They have short legs and can be used on the ground or on a heat-resistant surface at tabletop height.

The food that can be cooked on small portable barbecues is rather restricted. If you aspire to cooking a whole fish or a spit-roasted chicken, you will need to invest in a more sophisticated piece of equipment. The free-standing brazier types have an open grill and sometimes come with a wind shield, hood, and/or spit-roaster. They are fitted with wheels or detachable legs, and some models are portable, making them convenient to transport to a picnic. Make sure the legs are long enough for you to be able to cook comfortably; it is less back-breaking to squat on the ground than to be half bent over something that is not quite the right height for standing at.

The bulbous kettle barbecues have a domed lid that excludes air, thus reducing the risk of flare-up. The lid also deflects heat onto the food, resulting in quicker and more even cooking, and enabling larger pieces to be cooked with success. Though the rack on kettle barbecues is not adjustable, the firebox has vents that enable you to control the cooking temperature. An enameled finish is more durable than the heat-resistant paint that some models are treated with.

The pedestal or pillar types of barbecue have a firebed set above an integral flue. The flue is filled with newspaper, which is lit through a ventilation hole, preferably with a long match. The upward draft creates a powerful draw that quickly lights the fuel.

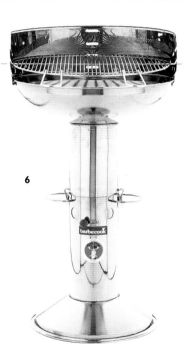

6

7

6 Pedestal barbecue This sleek, stainless-steel model is good-looking enough to grace the balcony of the most design-conscious loft dweller. No need for messy chopped kindling, just stuff the flue with yesterday's newspaper and ignite. Though there will be billowing smoke at first, it soon dies down. The barbecue has ventilation holes for regulating temperature, and a windshield with three slots for adjusting rack height. Drawbacks: the outer surface becomes intensely hot and is therefore a hazard to children and pets; the barbecue is tall and the base relatively narrow, so it must be set on very flat, level ground to remain stable.

7 Kettle barbecue An all-American classic, this outstanding barbecue is made in rust-resisting enameled steel, and has a thermometer in its lid for accurate monitoring of temperature. The vents open for cooking while the lid is lowered, creating convection heat that produces a tasty crisp exterior and seals in juices. A touch of a button conveniently releases ashes into a container below the firebox.

Successful barbecuing

O If possible, line the base of the firebox with foil and cover with sand. This absorbs fat drippings and helps prevent flare-up.

O Light the barbecue with good old-fashioned paper and sticks. Once lit, leave the charcoal alone until it is covered in pale gray ash. Only then is it ready to use.

O To assess temperature, hold your palm 6 inches from the grill and count. If you can feel the heat after 2 to 3 seconds, the fire is hot enough for cooking small thin items such as sausage links, skewered food, and fish fillets.

O If you can hold your hand over the grill for 4 to 5 seconds, the heat is suitable for larger pieces that need longer cooking such as chops, spareribs, or chicken quarters.

O If you can withstand the heat for longer than 5 seconds, the fire is not hot enough.

O Keep tools with extra-long handles within easy reach of the barbecue. You will need tongs, a fork, a spatula, and a brush. A pointed knife is useful to test for doneness.

O Keep one pair of tongs solely for transferring raw meat and poultry to the barbecue. This reduces the risk of food poisoning.

barbecued seafood skewers
with sun-dried tomato basil aïoli and grilled vegetable salad

Perfect for a summer lunch, this mouthwatering recipe was contributed by Wolfgang Puck, one of an influential breed of chefs who launched new trends in Californian cuisine with an expert blend of fresh local ingredients and classical French technique. Cook the vegetables first, then stoke up the barbecue so it is very hot before you grill the seafood.

Serves 6 to 8

Tools

cook's knife

mezzaluna

large, shallow dish

paring knife

food processor

6 metal skewers, about 12 inches long

Ingredients

1 lb. swordfish or salmon, cut into 1-inch cubes

1 lb. scallops, halved if large

1 lb. large, uncooked shrimp, shelled and deveined

salt

For the marinade:

1/2 cup olive oil

2 tbsp. freshly ground black pepper

1/4 cup finely chopped herbs, including basil, oregano, thyme, and parsley

For the sun-dried tomato basil aïoli:

1/3 cup sun-dried tomatoes, packed in oil

2 tbsp. chopped basil

8 garlic cloves, or 1 head, roasted

2 tbsp. balsamic vinegar

1/2 cup extra-virgin olive oil

salt and freshly ground black pepper

For the grilled vegetable salad:

8 oz. scallions or leeks, halved lengthways

8 oz. small carrots or either baby or regular corn cobs, halved lengthways

8 oz. zucchini, halved lengthways

8 oz. Japanese eggplants, halved lengthways

2 red bell peppers, halved and seeded

8 oz. fennel, cut lengthways into 1/2-inch thick slices

4 large tomatoes, halved and seeded

salt and freshly ground black pepper

1 cup olive oil

1 tbsp. finely chopped garlic

1 tsp. ground cumin

1/2 cup balsamic vinegar

1/2 coarsely chopped fresh herbs, including basil, oregano, parsley, and thyme

1 Mix all the marinade ingredients together. Put all the seafood in a large shallow dish and pour the marinade over. Refrigerate for 2 to 4 hours.

2 To make the aïoli, put the sun-dried tomatoes, basil, garlic, and balsamic vinegar in a food processor and purée until smooth. With the motor still running, slowly add the olive oil and season with salt and pepper. Refrigerate until ready for use.

3 For the grilled vegetable salad, mix all the vegetables with salt, pepper, and half the olive oil. Place on a hot barbecue and grill until tender and brown (some vegetables may take longer than others). Remove from the grill, cool and cut into 1-inch pieces. Cut the tomatoes into 1/2-inch cubes and add to the vegetables. Mix the vegetables with the garlic, cumin, vinegar, herbs, and remaining olive oil.

4 When ready to cook the seafood, thread onto skewers, alternating shrimp, scallops, and swordfish or salmon (about 6 oz. per skewer). Season each skewer with salt.

5 When the barbecue is very hot, grill the seafood for about 4 minutes on each side.

6 To serve, divide the vegetable salad between individual plates and place a skewer on top of the salad. Drizzle part of the aïoli over the seafood and serve the rest on the side.

slightly smoky grilled quails
with ginger, mirin, basil, and sesame

At London's famous Sugar Club restaurant, brilliant New Zealand chef Peter Gordon combines modern British food with the very best of Pacific Rim flavors. His quail recipe is perfect for the barbecue. As he says, "Quails are great to barbecue because they're easy to hold in your hands, and they'll dribble just the right amount of juice down your chin." Though not essential, a barbecue with a lid allows the quails to take on a smoky flavor without burning.

Serves 4

Tools	Ingredients
kitchen scissors	8 quails
large bowl	a good handful of basil leaves, plus a little extra, shredded
paring knife	
long-handled tongs or fork	3 tbsp. plus 1 tsp. sesame oil
citrus juicer	2 tsp. sesame seeds
	thumb-sized piece fresh gingerroot, very finely chopped
	3 garlic cloves, finely chopped
	4 tsp. Thai fish sauce
	4 tsp. mirin
	4 tsp. wine vinegar
	1 tbsp. demerara sugar
	lime juice, to taste

1 Hold a quail in your hand, breast-side down, and cut out the backbone with a pair of kitchen scissors (see "spatchcocked poussins," page 26). Put the bird in a large bowl. Repeat with the others.

2 Add the remaining ingredients to the bowl, reserving some of the basil, and toss together. Cover with plastic wrap and leave to marinate in the refrigerator for at least 6 hours. Remove from the refrigerator about 2 hours before you're ready to cook, so the birds have time to come to room temperature.

3 Once the barbecue coals are glowing, make them into a mound in the center. Lay the quails, flattened out and breast-side up, on the rack in a ring around this hot mound. Close the lid if you have one, as this will keep some of the heat and the smoke in. Cook for 6 minutes, then open the lid, turn over the quails, close the lid again, and cook for another 5 to 8 minutes.

4 Test a quail by poking its thigh with a sharp knife at the thickest point. If the juices run clear, it's cooked. If they are still pink, continue to cook for a couple more minutes, then test again. If the bird is black and flaming, you'll be going hungry.

5 Transfer the cooked quails to a platter and sprinkle with the extra shredded basil and a squeeze of lime.

tools for lifting and turning

When maneuvering food at high temperatures, you need long-handled tools to protect your hands. The tools should grip well or be shaped in such a way that they are compatible with the nature of the food and/or the shape of the pan. Hang them within easy reach of the stovetop so you don't have to fumble in a drawer. Avoid lifters and turners with wooden or painted handles, and those with rivets and joins. A continuous piece of metal is easier to clean and will last a lifetime.

1 Fish lifter This efficient tool enables you to lift a whole fish and keep it intact. The bowed blade has a gently chamfered edge that slips easily under the fish without tearing the skin. The perforations allow fat to drain.

2 Wok turner The rapid stirring, turning and lifting of food that stir-frying demands are made simple with this shovel-shaped tool. It is available with or without perforations.

3 Fish turner A thin, rounded blade allows careful handling of fish and other delicate foods. The slots make the blade flexible and allow fat to drain away as you lift.

4 Spring-action tongs Popular with professional cooks, these stainless-steel tongs have a positive spring action and ample scalloped heads that allow you to clasp food securely.

5 Scissor-action tongs With their inwardly curved, pincerlike heads, these tongs are ideal for lifting and turning small pieces of food. The plastic-coated handles are comfortable to hold and remain cool during use.

6 Angled turner Ergonomically designed for comfort, this angled turner is available in right- and left-handed versions.

7 Nonstick turner Even though nonstick pans are more durable than they used to be, it still makes sense to use a nonstick turner. This one is made of die-cast aluminum and has

8 Bamboo rice paddle and fork These are used for serving rice or mixing it with other ingredients. The paddle's tapered edge separates rice grains without crushing them.

9 Wire scoop This is ideal for scooping up french fries, sauté potatoes, and any deep-fried food. Oil quickly drains away through the coarse wire mesh. The scoop also makes a useful skimmer.

10 Turning fork A five-pronged fork delicately harpoons slippery food.

roasting stewing and baking

roasting

Look for good, solid roasting pans and be prepared to pay for them—the one that came with your oven will inevitably warp and you'll end up with the fat gathering in one corner, leaving the rest of the pan high and dry.

Roasting pans come in a variety of materials. However, size and weight are more important. Pans need at least 2 inches of space around them for air to circulate, so check the size of your oven before buying. Get several sizes—if you roast a small piece of meat in too large a pan, the juices will spread thinly and burn. Conversely, a large roast or bird in an undersized pan will cook unevenly. Pans should be rigid, with sides high enough to restrict splattering. Sizeable roasts can be heavy, so when choosing a large pan, make sure it has handles or a flat rim you can grip easily. A nonstick surface is worth having if you are trying to reduce your fat intake. If you like roasted vegetables, get a large shallow-edged pan too. It will double as a cookie sheet.

I Double oven mitts All-in-one oven mitts are easier to use, store, and find than a pair. The deep pockets are triple-lined on the palm side and double-lined on the back, protecting your hands and wrists even if you happen to brush against the inside of the oven

3 Anodized aluminum roasting pan This heavy-duty roasting pan and the shallow roasting tray (4) are guaranteed not to twist or buckle when they are exposed to high temperatures. The hard surface is resistant to scratches, even from metal utensils. The base is solid enough to stand up to the direct heat of the stovetop, so you can use the pan for making gravy. This roasting pan is available in a range of sizes and will last a lifetime.

4 Lifting forks A pair of lifting forks ease the transfer of meat from roasting pan to serving platter. Choose forks that have at least three prongs. Any fewer and the meat is in danger of dropping between them.

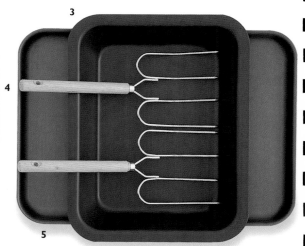

2 Enameled self-basting roaster This cleverly designed, high-quality roaster has a series of dimples set into the lid. These encourage moisture to gather and drip evenly over the meat, resulting in a particularly succulent roast.

The steel rack lifts the meat out of the fat. Because the meat is completely enclosed, its surface will not become crisp. If you want it to be crisp, remove the lid toward the end of the cooking time.

5 Anodized aluminum roasting tray The ideal pan for roasting vegetables. Sliced eggplant, onion rings, and bell peppers, for example, will become deliciously crisp and sticky as the dry heat of the oven circulates over them, unimpeded by a high-sided pan. The generous surface area means you can give your vegetables plenty of room. If you cram them together they will simply steam in their own juices and remain pallid.

6 Fat separators As cooking fat always rises to the top as it cools, a utensil with a spout that joins the jug at the base allows you to draw off liquid, leaving the fat behind. Elegant enough to be brought to the table, the porcelain fat separator (left) is ingeniously designed to pour fat-free gravy from a deep spout at one end, and the risen fat from a shallow spout at the other. The more functional-looking acrylic fat separator (right) is available in 1-quart and 1½-cup sizes, and can be used for gravy, soup, or stock.

7 Vertical chicken roaster Cut down on roasting time with this vertical roaster, which is designed to conduct heat directly to the inside of the bird. The bird browns and crisps evenly, while fat and juices drain into the pan base.

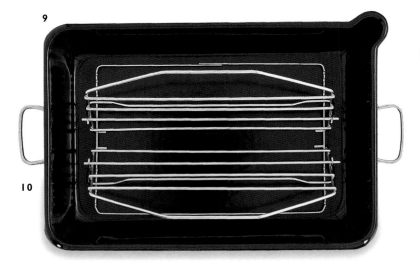

6

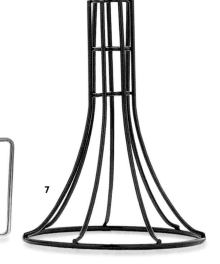

7

8

8 Trussing needle Resembling a giant darning needle with an eye large enough to take a piece of string, a trussing needle makes a more secure job of sealing flaps and openings in poultry or tying a roast into a neat, compact shape. Unlike a skewer, it can pass all the way through the meat, drawing the string with it.

9 Enameled roasting pan This heavy-duty pan measures 15 × 10 inches and is perfect for large roasts. Sturdy handles assist with lifting and fold out of the way so they don't take up space in the oven. A lip in one corner accurately directs fat and juices as you pour them off. The enameled surface is smooth and easy to clean.

11 Bulb baster Rather surgical in appearance, this glass tube and rubber squeeze ball is used for basting as well as drawing off fat. Fill the tube with meat juices by squeezing the ball, then release and hold the tube upright. The fat will rise to the top and the fat-free juices can be squirted over the meat or used to make a gravy or sauce. Calibrations show exactly how much liquid the tube has sucked up, which can be useful in sauce-making.

9

10

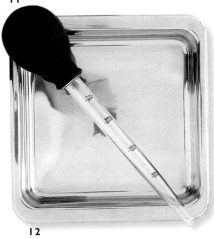

11

12

10 V-shaped roasting rack Fully adjustable, this rack lifts any size of bird or roast well away from the base of the pan. Ordinary flat racks do little more than raise the meat an inch above the pan, which is of little use if you are cooking a goose or a duck, for example, as they produce copious amounts of fat. The v-shape not only facilitates clearance of fat but allows air to circulate under the meat, resulting in faster, more even cooking and crisper skins.

12 Stainless-steel mini roasting pan People who live on their own need not deprive themselves of the pleasure of a roast. Just 8 inches square, this pan is the perfect size for one. It is also useful for roasting whole onions, beets, or turnips. Made of top-grade stainless steel, it can also be used under the broiler and on the stovetop.

pork and crackling

Jamie Oliver is one of Britain's most talented young chefs, and this recipe perfectly captures his feisty, no-fuss style. Boneless pork is roasted flat, directly on the bars of the oven shelf, with a roasting pan beneath to catch the juices. This produces succulent meat, the crispest, crunchiest crackling ever, and gravy that will have you licking your plate. Ask your butcher to take the meat off the bone and then to score the skin across in deep lines about ¼-inch apart. Ask for the bones to be chopped up so you can use them to make the gravy.

Serves 8

Tools	Ingredients
mortar and pestle	½ pork top loin, 6½ lb. on the bone
large roasting pan	sea salt flakes
medium roasting tray for browning bones	1 tbsp. chopped fresh rosemary
aluminum foil	½ tbsp. fennel seeds
large skillet or saucepan for making gravy	5 cloves garlic
wooden spoon	8 tbsp. balsamic vinegar
sieve	4 bay leaves
	2 tbsp. olive oil
	pork bones, chopped
	5 outer celery sticks, roughly chopped
	1 large carrot, roughly chopped
	1 large onion, roughly chopped

1 Rub some salt and rosemary into the pork skin, pushing it into the scored lines.

2 Using a mortar and pestle, smash up the fennel seeds, then the garlic and remaining rosemary. Rub this mixture into the meat—not the skin, or it will burn. Place the meat in a large roasting pan with the balsamic vinegar, bay leaves, and olive oil. Leave for about 30 minutes to marinate.

3 Heat the oven to its highest temperature and brown the bones. Rub the pork skin with more salt.

4 Place the pork directly onto the bars at the top of the oven. Put the browned bones and vegetables in the roasting pan with the leftover balsamic marinade and add 2½ cups of water. Set the pan in the oven directly under the pork, so that as the pork cooks, all the juices drip from it into the pan. This liquid will then become your gravy. You also get quite nice charred bar marks on the base of the pork.

5 The pork will take about 1 hour to cook. After 20 minutes, turn the temperature down to 425°F. Once the pork is cooked, remove it from the oven on the rack and place on a piece of foil to save any juices. Allow to rest for at least 10 minutes so the juices flow through the meat, making it more tender.

6 To make the gravy, put the bones, liquid, and vegetables from the roasting pan into a large skillet or saucepan. Add some water to the roasting pan, as there will be some sticky stuff on the bottom of the pan, which is very tasty. Bring to a boil on the stovetop, scraping all the flavorful bits from the bottom of the roasting pan, then add this to the bones and vegetables.

7 Bring the gravy to a boil, stirring occasionally. Remove any oil or scum from the surface, then strain the contents, discarding all the vegetables and bones. You can reduce and then adjust the seasoning to taste.

honey-glazed roast barbary duck

Barbary ducks are not so fatty as ordinary ducks and have more flesh on the breast. Repeated brushing with a fragrant coating produces a wonderfully crisp skin with a deep, rich glaze. Allow several hours for the duck to dry; you can speed things up with a cool hair-dryer if necessary. This is delicious served with julienned leeks and carrots, and "mashed sweet potatoes" (see page 40).

Serves 3 to 4

Tools	Ingredients
colander	1 barbary duck, weighing 3 1/2 to 4 lb.
paring knife	20 to 25 thin shreds orange peel, about 1/2-inch long
mortar and pestle	1/3 cup honey
ginger grater	4 tbsp. rice wine or dry sherry
wire rack set over a shallow dish	4 tbsp. white-wine vinegar
wide, flat brush	4 tbsp. soy sauce
12- x 10-inch roasting pan with rack	2 tsp. fennel seeds, ground to a powder
lifting forks	1 1/2-inch piece fresh gingerroot, peeled and grated
carving knife	2 tsp. sesame oil
poultry shears	3/4 cup plus 2 tbsp. homemade duck or chicken stock
small saucepan	sea salt and freshly ground black pepper

1 Discard any lumps of fat from the duck's cavity. Put the duck in a colander and scald all over with boiling water. Pat dry thoroughly with a paper towel. Pierce the flesh evenly all over with the tip of a knife and insert the orange-peel shreds. Place the duck on a rack set over a dish.

2 Pour the honey into a small measuring jug. Stir in the rice wine or dry sherry, vinegar, soy sauce, fennel seeds, gingerroot, and sesame oil. Paint the mixture over the entire surface of the duck, including the crevices under the wings; reserve the remainder. Leave the duck on the rack in a cool, airy place to dry completely.

3 Preheat the oven to 425°F. Brush the duck once more, using the liquid that has dripped into the dish.

4 Place the duck, breast-side up, on a rack in a roasting pan. Roast for 10 minutes, then turn the duck over, brush again with the coating mixture, and roast for another 10 minutes.

5 Reduce the heat to 375°F. Turn the duck breast-side up, brush, and roast for 30 minutes. Turn and roast for another 30 minutes, brushing every 10 minutes. Protect any blackened tips with foil.

6 Raise the heat to 400°F and turn the duck breast-side up. Brush again and roast for 10 minutes more. Lift the duck onto a heated dish and leave to rest in a warm place for 10 minutes.

7 To carve the duck, remove the legs and the wings, leaving some of the breast meat attached to each wing. Remove the breast meat in two long pieces, then cut into bite-size chunks, making sure a crispy piece of skin is attached to each chunk. Place all the duck pieces in a shallow serving dish and keep warm.

8 Pour any juices that have accumulated during carving into a small saucepan. Add the stock and the remaining coating. Simmer briskly until slightly reduced. Pour over the duck pieces and serve.

pots for braising and stewing

These pots form the backbone of any kitchen. They competently brown and simmer fragrant braises and stews, and come in all shapes and sizes, each with special characteristics. Materials are the same as those used for saucepans (see "material choice," page 8), with the addition of ceramic. However, unlike saucepans these pots have small, ear-shaped handles.

The ideal pot is one you can use on the stovetop or in the oven, and that is good looking enough to bring to the table. It is useful to have at least one pot that can be transferred from freezer to oven. You will need a couple of cooking pots, either in cast iron or stainless steel, for everyday use; a 6½-quart pot serves 4 to 5 people, and a 3¼-quart pot serves 2 to 3 people. A shallow braising pan with a lid is also likely to earn its keep for big weekend breakfasts and for slow-cooked braises. A Dutch oven is a must for pot roasts and stews. Sizes range from a minuscule 2¼ quarts to a vat-like 13½ quarts. Though it may seem unnecessarily large, the 9- to 10-quart size is well worth having—it can always double up as a soup, stock, or even a pasta pot.

1 Braising pan This braiser can be used on the stovetop or in the oven. The domed lid encourages condensation and maintains moist heat within the pot. Without the lid, the braiser can be used for frying. Made of 18/10 stainless steel, with a thick aluminum core extending up the sides of the pan, it conducts heat quickly and evenly.

2 Brittany pot Classic French dishes such as moules à la marinières, as well as stews and braises, are traditionally prepared in these rounded pots with gently flaring sides. Made of enamelled cast iron, this one comes in four colors.

3 Tagine A tagine is a uniquely shaped, thick earthenware pot, used in North Africa for the slow-cooked dish of the same name. The pot is traditionally used on an open fire. Very little liquid is needed as the conical lid provides a large cool surface on which steam condenses and then drips onto the food below. The tall shape also keeps the lid cool at the top, so it can be lifted without a protective cloth.

Modified for use on the stovetop, this tagine has an enameled cast-iron base that maintains even heat at low temperatures; it can be used on any type of stovetop. The earthenware lid is glazed inside and out, making it durable and easy to clean.

4 French oven This magnificent 6½-quart cooking pot is made of 18/10 stainless steel with an aluminum inner core for optimum heat conductivity. The core extends all the way up the sides of the pan (see "material choice," stainless steel, page 8). The pot comes with an internal rack for easy removal of contents. It has ear-shaped, stay-cool handles.

5 Nonstick casserole Made of titanium, the surface of this casserole is hard enough to withstand the use of metal tools. A rock-solid base browns and crisps at high temperatures but is equally good for gentle simmering. The glass lid, sold separately, is heat resistant up to 540°F so can be used in an oven. It is suitable for all stovetops except the induction type.

Terminology

O **Braising** A moist cooking method in which food is placed in a covered dish with just enough liquid to produce steam during cooking.

O **Casserole** This term refers to oven-baked food that is bound with a sauce and cooked in a casserole or Dutch oven.

O **Pot roasting** This is a similar technique to braising, but relies more on moisture from the vegetables and meat being cooked than on added liquid.

O **Stewing** A slow, moist cooking method for tough meats and for developing rich flavors. Just enough liquid is added to cover the ingredients.

6 Enameled Dutch oven Also known as a "cocotte," this very heavy, enameled cast-iron pot has tall, straight sides for holding substantial quantities of meat, vegetables, and liquid. The heavy lid can either be sealed with a strip of dough or set slightly askew to allow steam to escape. A thick base allows for even heat transference on the stovetop. Use it for browning and slowly simmering stews.

7 Cast-iron Dutch oven This handsome pot in pre-seasoned, black cast iron was designed by Björn Dahlström and is destined to become a modern classic. Like the traditional Dutch oven, it has a thick, flat base for browning, and tall sides for holding a large volume of meat and liquid. The sides flare slightly to encourage evaporation. It is available in a 5 1/2-quart size only.

8 Brushed stainless-steel casserole Another modern classic by Björn Dahlström, this pot has the same minimalist lines as the cast-iron Dutch oven. Available in 5 1/2- and 8 3/4-quart sizes, it is made of superior 18/10 stainless steel with a thick aluminum core that extends all the way up the sides, giving good heat distribution throughout the pan.

9 Polished stainless-steel casserole Designed by Robert Welch, this gleaming pan combines looks with functionality. The base has a thick copper core for fast, even heat distribution, and the handles are set away from the pan for safety and comfort (use oven mitts after prolonged cooking). The lid is reversible for efficient storage and stacking. The casserole is available in 3-, 4 1/2-, and 6 1/3-quart sizes.

clay pots

Together with iron, clay was one of the earliest materials used for making cooking pots, dating back to primitive times when food was cooked over an open fire or a bed of hot ashes. As their origin suggests, these homely pots are designed for simmering over a low gas flame or in the oven. Whatever their shape—tall, shallow, straight, or bulbous—their virtue is that they absorb heat slowly and evenly, so food cooks uniformly without burning or drying out.

All clay pots are brittle, their strength depending on the temperature at which they were fired. The higher the temperature, the stronger the pot. The most brittle, and cheapest, are earthenware pots.

Glazed clay pots are nonporous, easier to clean, and retain heat better than unglazed ones. Conversely, an unglazed surface absorbs heat more readily, so choose one with an unglazed base.

1 Bean pot/fait tout This solid, spacious, 4½-quart pot truly lives up to its French name ("fait tout" meaning "does all"). The bulging sides increase both the capacity and the actual heating surface, while the slightly narrower neck helps to slow evaporation. The bean pot is resistant to thermal shock so it can be transferred directly from the freezer to the oven. It is also dishwasher-proof.

2 Marmite The tall, partially glazed marmite is traditionally used for hearty stews such as cassoulet or pot-au-feu. The lid is domed, which allows condensation to drip back into the pot and keep the contents moist. When the lid is removed, the large surface area created by the wide diameter and straight sides encourages evaporation and the formation of the authentic cassoulet crust.

3 Oval terrine An oval is a traditional shape for making and serving a rustic terrine or pâté of ground meat or fish. The tightly-fitting lid rests on an inner lip and prevents food from drying out. Some terrines have a lid with a hole for steam to escape. The pot can also be used for stews. It is dishwasher-proof, and can withstand temperatures from −4°F to 480°F.

4 Tontopf pot This unglazed pot is designed for making deliciously moist, oven-cooked stews with almost no water or fat. Before cooking, the entire pot is soaked in cold water, which is released as steam as the pot heats up. The steam condenses inside the lid and moisture drips onto the food.

5 Round terracotta pot Fired at 1920°F, this classic, straight-sided, glazed pot is resistant to fracturing and fluctuations of temperature. It is ideal for a winter meal for two, or for reheating small portions of leftover stew. It also makes an individual oven-to-table serving dish for hearty soups that need finishing off in the oven—onion soup, for example.

chicken tagine with preserved lemons

This wonderfully fragrant recipe was contributed by Claudia Roden, the acclaimed food writer who is credited with having "single-handedly introduced the Western palate to Middle Eastern cuisine." The word "tagine" refers to both the stew and the pot in which it is cooked. The tagine pot (see page 102) gives the best results, but you can use a flameproof casserole into which the chicken fits snugly. If you use an earthenware tagine, there is a danger that it will crack if set over a gas flame. A heat diffuser will help prevent this; alternatively, do the preliminary cooking in a saucepan, then transfer the chicken to the earthenware pot and finish cooking in the oven.

Serves 4 to 6

Tools	Ingredients
grater	1 chicken, weighing about 4 lb.
garlic press	1 onion, grated or very finely chopped
mortar and pestle	2 garlic cloves, crushed
mezzaluna or cook's knife	1/4 tsp. saffron pistils, crushed
tagine or 4.2-quart round or oval flameproof Dutch oven	1/2 tsp. ground ginger
	1 1/2 tsp. ground cinnamon
2 large metal spoons	salt and freshly ground black pepper
cook's knife	large bunch cilantro, trimmed and finely chopped
	large bunch flat-leaf parsley, trimmed and finely chopped
	peel of 1 1/2 preserved lemons (see below), cut into quarters
	3 oz. green olives, soaked in 2 changes of water for 30 minutes, drained and rinsed

1 Put the chicken in a tagine or casserole with all the ingredients except the preserved lemons and olives. Half cover with water (about 1 1/4 cups) and simmer on a medium to low heat, covered, for 1 hour, turning the chicken over a few times and adding more water if necessary.

2 Throw the lemon peel and olives into the sauce and continue to simmer for 20 minutes, or until the chicken is so tender the flesh pulls off the bone and the liquid is reduced.

3 Lift the chicken from the sauce and place in a shallow dish. Cut into serving-size pieces and place in a serving dish or the base of a tagine. Using paper towels, blot any oil from the surface of the sauce. Pour the sauce over the chicken. Serve with couscous if you like.

Preserved lemons Wash and scrub four thick-skinned lemons. Cut into quarters lengthways but stop short at the stem end so the pieces are still attached. Stuff each lemon with 1 tablespoon of sea salt. Pack into a clean glass jar into which the lemons will just fit, pressing so they are squashed together. Seal the jar and leave for three or four days. They will start to release their juices and the skins will soften. Press them down as much as possible, and add enough fresh lemon juice to completely cover them. Seal the jar and leave in a cool place for at least a month. Rinse before using, to get rid of the salt.

beef pot roast with winter vegetables

Long, slow cooking in the moist environment of a covered pot produces meltingly tender meat from even the cheapest cuts. The meat is first browned and then gently cooked with vegetables and a relatively small amount of liquid. It bubbles away lazily, enriching the liquid in which it sits, and leaving you free to get on with other things. A sprinkling of finely chopped parsley, lemon zest, and garlic added just before serving gives a lovely fresh flavor to the dish.

Serves 4

Tools	Ingredients
paring knife	3¹/₂ to 4 lb. rolled beef, brisket
Dutch oven into which the meat fits snugly	4 fat garlic cloves, thinly sliced, plus 1 small garlic clove, finely chopped
tongs	
cook's knife	about 20 rosemary leaves
vegetable peeler	2 tbsp. vegetable oil
citrus grater	2 tbsp. butter
mezzaluna	1 red onion, finely chopped
conical sieve	2 celery sticks, finely diced
4 saucepans	2 carrots, finely diced
whisk	small bunch of thyme
carving knife	1 bay leaf
	2 or 3 strips thinly pared orange peel
	1¹/₂ cups red wine
	²/₃ cup meat stock, preferably homemade
	sea salt and freshly ground black pepper
	finely grated zest of 1 lemon
	3 tbsp. chopped flat-leaf parsley
	¹/₂ tbsp. plain flour
	To serve:
	16 baby carrots
	12 small potatoes, shaped into ovals
	1 Savoy cabbage, quartered and cut into ribbons
	knob of butter

1 Heat the oven to 275°F. Dry the meat thoroughly and make slits all over it with the tip of a small knife. Poke pieces of sliced garlic and the rosemary leaves into the slits, using the knife tip to embed them (a).

2 Heat the vegetable oil in a Dutch oven. When it is very hot, add the meat and brown on all sides, turning with tongs (b). Transfer the meat to a plate.

3 Add half the butter to the pot. When it is sizzling, add the onion, celery, and carrots and gently fry for about 5 minutes until soft.

4 Put the meat back in the pot, together with any juices that have accumulated. Add the thyme, bay leaf, and orange peel, then pour in the wine and stock (c). The liquid should come no more than one-third of the way up the meat. Season with salt and freshly ground black pepper.

5 Bring the liquid to a boil, then cover with a tight-fitting lid and put in the oven. Cook for 3 to 3¹/₂ hours, turning every 30 minutes or so.

6 Toward the end of the cooking time, mix together the lemon zest, parsley, and chopped garlic. Mix the flour and remaining butter to a smooth paste. Cook the carrots, potatoes, and cabbage until tender but still crisp and brightly colored. Keep them warm in separate saucepans.

7 Remove the meat from the pot. Put it in a warm dish and leave to rest in a warm place for 10 minutes, loosely covered with foil.

8 Meanwhile, blot up any fat from the braising liquid with paper towels. Strain the vegetables into a saucepan, pressing them with the back of a spoon to extract all the liquid.

9 Bring the strained liquid to the boil, adding any juices that have flowed from the meat. Whisk in small pieces of the butter and flour paste, continuing to whisk until the sauce is smooth.

10 Carve the meat and arrange in overlapping slices on a warm serving platter. Pour the sauce over the meat and sprinkle with the most of the parsley mixture.

11 Warm the vegetables through with butter, season with sea salt and freshly ground black pepper, and sprinkle with the remaining parsley.

baking and gratin dishes

These dishes are designed for baking food in the oven or browning toppings of bubbling cheese, crisp potato, or crunchy bread crumbs. Made of good-quality materials, such as porcelain or cast iron, gratin dishes conduct heat well and are not stressed by high temperatures. They are usually brought to the table so are made in attractive shapes and colors.

1 Rectangular ceramic gratin dishes These glazed dishes are strong enough to be transferred directly from freezer to oven. The rectangular shape makes efficient use of oven and refrigerator space, while gently sloping sides maximize the area for crusty topping and also allow stacking. A thick rim assists with lifting.

The large gratin dish is deep enough to take four or five layers of lasagna. The slightly rounded interior makes serving and cleaning easier.

2 Oval ceramic gratin dishes These are the classic shape for a gratin and are versatile enough to be used as serving dishes, or even for carving a small roast. The dishes can be transferred directly from freezer to oven. They conduct heat evenly and retain it well, ensuring food remains warm at the table.

3 Porcelain soufflé dishes Round, deep, and straight sided, these dishes expose soufflé mixtures to maximum heat. This coagulates the egg proteins before the air incorporated during whisking has time to escape. The smooth porcelain interior allows the expanding mixture to rise up the dish. It is available in several sizes, but the preferred one is 1 quart. Anything larger and you risk the inside not being properly cooked.

4 Enameled cast-iron egg dish This shallow dish is specially designed for cooking eggs, either in the oven or on the stovetop. Widely flaring sides make serving and cleaning easier, but more importantly they increase the surface area and expose the eggs to maximum heat so they cook evenly.

5 Enameled cast-iron baking dish The deep sides of this dish make it particularly useful for baking eggs that have a layer of vegetables, such as spinach, underneath, or for individual portions of lasagne.

6 Porcelain ramekins These smooth, straight-sided ramekins are used for individual soufflés, as well as baked custards or crème brûlées. Egg-based dishes such as these are cooked in a roasting pan filled with enough hot water to come halfway up the sides of the ramekins. The ramekins have a slightly roughened base to prevent a vacuum from forming and making it hard to lift them from the water bath.

7 Porcelain oval gratin dishes Available in several sizes, these classic white gratin dishes have a beautiful shape. The fluted handles merge with the sides of the dish, which slope gracefully outwards to increase the surface area for browning. The sloping sides increase the surface area.

8 Porcelain chocolate pots These elegant pots are traditionally used for rich chocolate desserts, as well as baked creams and custards.

Gratin dishes are shallow so they fit under the broiler or close to the top of the oven. Handles are small and project outward rather than upward so food can be positioned close to the broiler. Some dishes have a rim around the top edge to make them easy to grasp while wearing an oven mitt.

The most indispensable dishes to have are a set of small, medium, and large ceramic gratin dishes, either rectangular or square. They will earn their keep by doubling as serving dishes for vegetables, rice, and salads. A set of six or eight individual-sized ramekins is also useful, not only for sweet or savory baked dishes, but also for serving small snacks to go with drinks.

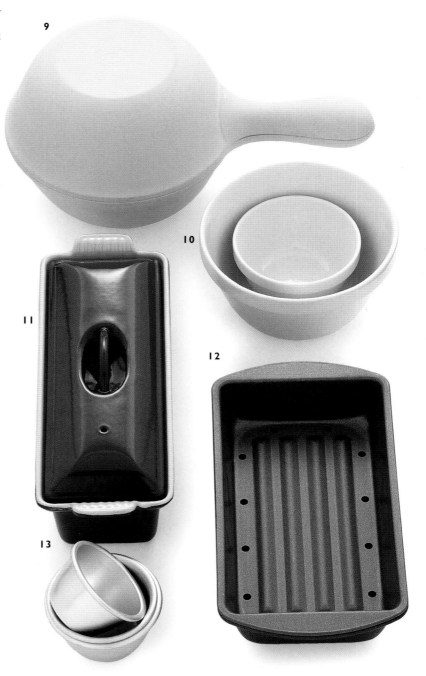

9 Earthenware potato baker
Known in France as a "diable," this porous, unglazed earthenware baker seals in moisture and effectively steam-cooks the contents. By doing so it conserves both flavor and aroma. To work well, the size and shape of the baker should closely follow those of the contents. There are different shaped bakers for cooking chicken and fish.

10 Glazed earthenware bowls
These are the classic bowls for steamed puddings. The mixture is covered with pleated waxed paper, held in place with string tied under the thick rim, which is designed for the purpose. These bowls are also ideal for chilled summer puddings, and can double as mixing bowls.

11 Cast-iron rectangular terrine
This dish is designed for baking and shaping the dense mixture of finely chopped vegetables, meat, or fish that constitutes a terrine. Cast iron permits the necessary slow, even cooking, while the elongated shape facilitates slicing the terrine into neat, cracker-sized portions.

12 Nonstick steel meat loaf pan
This two-part pan has a ridged, perforated base for draining away the fatty liquid that is the bane of cooking a meat loaf. The outer pan doubles as a bread pan.

13 Aluminum pudding bowls
These bowls can be used for steamed puddings, and as cold molds for chilled custards and mousses. Aluminum is not a suitable material for cooking fruit desserts unless lined with waxed paper (see "material choice," page 8).

fresh shell bean gratin

Alice Waters is one of America's favorite chefs. Described as "poetic," "visionary," and "passionate," her cooking is based on the belief that optimal flavor and environmental harmony go hand in hand. This comforting dish is typical of her cooking. You will need a gratin dish about 2 inches deep and 9 inches square. Fresh shell beans are available in late summer and early fall. Use a mixture of beans of varying colors. You will need 2 to 3 lb. in their pods, which should provide 1 to 1¼ lb. when shelled. You can also make the gratin with dried beans. Soak 1¼ cups of beans (separately, if using a mixture) overnight. Drain and boil rapidly in fresh water for 20 minutes. Drain again and begin cooking with step 1.

Serves 4 to 6

Tools	Ingredients
medium-size saucepans for each type of bean	1 to 1¼ lb. podded fresh shell beans, such as cannellini, flageolet, and borlotti
strainer	
jug or bowl	
cook's knife	salt
paring knife	6 tbsp. olive oil
medium skillet	½ onion, finely chopped
wooden spoon	
1½-quart gratin dish	4 garlic cloves, cut into slivers
	1 or 2 sage leaves, chopped
	4 to 5 oz. greens such as chard, broccoli raab, mustard greens, turnip tops, sliced into ribbons (optional)
	2 tomatoes, roughly chopped
	½ cup toasted bread crumbs (see below)

1 Put the beans in a saucepan with just enough water to cover by 1 inch (fresh shell beans absorb very little water). When they have come to the boil, add salt and 2 tablespoons of the olive oil, and lower the heat to a simmer. Cook until the beans are tender, about 30 minutes. Drain the beans in a strainer set over a measuring jug, and save their liquid.

2 Heat the oven to 350°F. While the beans are cooking, gently fry the onion in 2 tablespoons of olive oil, with the garlic, sage leaves, and some salt, until the onion is soft and translucent. If you wish, cook a small bunch of greens with the onion; add a little of the bean water along with them if you do.

3 When the onion is cooked, add the tomatoes, raise the heat, and cook for a minute or two more.

4 Combine the beans in a gratin dish with the onions, tomatoes, and greens, if using. Add enough bean water to almost cover. Taste, correct the seasoning, and pour the rest of the olive oil over the gratin.

5 Cover the top with toasted bread crumbs and bake for 45 minutes. Check occasionally and moisten with more bean water if the gratin seems to be drying out too much.

Toasted bread crumbs Heat the oven to 300°F. Remove the crust from stale levain bread or other country-style bread. Shred into small pieces and either chop it by hand or in a food processor, or leave in rough chunks depending on use. Toss with a pinch of salt and a little olive oil to coat the bread. Spread the crumbs on a baking sheet in a thin layer. Bake until golden brown, tossing every 10 minutes.

dough
making

tools for pizza and pasta

There is no mystique to making the dough for these all-time comforters—just chemistry, patience, and a sense of touch. The most important piece of equipment is your hands. Other tools just help things along.

For success with homemade pizza dough, bake your pizza on a baking stone preheated in an oven set at the highest temperature possible. With luck, the result will match the deliciously crisp crust produced by the intense heat of a wood-fired brick oven.

Making your own pasta dough takes time but is a particularly relaxing and satisfying experience. The result will be far superior to the so-called "fresh" pasta sold by supermarkets.

1 Perforated pizza pan The holes in this pan allow heat and air to reach the center of the dough, resulting in a crisper crust than is possible with a solid cookie sheet. The pan is particularly good for large pizzas.

2 Pizza stone Preheated in a very hot oven, this thick, unglazed ceramic slab draws moisture from the dough, producing a crisp yet chewy crust. It comes in diameters of 12 to 16 inches.

3 Pizza peel/paddle This flat tool has a chamfered edge that slides smoothly under a pizza as you lift it from the stone. Peels are also made of wood, which remains cooler in use.

4 Ravioli tray Made of cast aluminum, this 36-square tray produces ravioli of a uniform size and shape. The wide, flat edges between the indentations increase the area of contact between the layers of dough and reduce the risk of leaks.

5 Pasta machine This hand-cranked pasta machine speeds the process of rolling and cutting dough. The machine has graduated openings that are used successively to reduce the dough to the desired thickness. Attachable cutters slice it into ribbons of different widths.

6 Wooden rollers These pleasing wooden rollers are deeply etched for hand-cutting dough into ribbons of various widths. The cutting edges are quite fragile and may chip if not handled with care.

7 Pasta cutting wheels This superb hand-crafted tool has two detachable brass wheels—one plain and one zigzagged for cutting saw-edged ribbons or ravioli. Unlike mass-produced cutters, the wheels have well-defined edges that produce a very clean cut. Being thick and heavy, brass remains cooler in use than lighter metals. This also contributes to a clean cut.

8 Ravioli cutter If you like extra-large pillows of ravioli, this 2¹/₂-inch square cutter, made of cast aluminum, is the tool to use.

fresh pasta

Making fresh pasta is really no more of a challenge than making pastry, especially if you use a machine to help you thin and cut the dough. The secret is in the kneading and gradual thinning. You must close the rollers a notch at a time, resisting any temptation to skip a notch.

Pasta responds to warmth so never work it on a marble or metal surface. Use a large wooden board or other smooth, relatively warm material. You need plenty of space for laying out the strips of pasta, and plenty of clean, dry dishcloths on which to lay them.

For the best results use Italian '00' flour, allowing $2/3$ cup for each extra large egg. That said, it is almost impossible to predict exactly how much flour will be needed. You need enough to produce a dough that is neither too dry nor too sticky. Start off with a little less flour—you can always add more. If you add it all at once and the dough is too dry, you will have to start again.

Makes enough for 4 to 6 servings

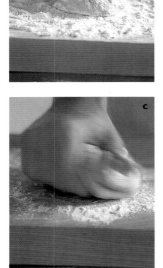

Tools	Ingredients
large wooden board	2 cups Italian '00' flour
dough scraper	(available from Italian delis)
hand-cranked pasta machine	3 extra large eggs, at room temperature

1 Pour the flour onto a wooden surface, shaping it into a mound with a central well. Break the eggs into the well and beat lightly with a fork. When evenly mixed, start drawing some of the flour over the eggs (a). Continue until the eggs are no longer runny.

2 Quickly draw the sides of the mound over the eggs, leaving a little flour on the side to use if the dough is too sticky. Work the eggs and flour together until smoothly integrated, adding the reserved flour if necessary (b). Wrap the dough in plastic wrap and scrape the surface clean.

3 Knead the dough by pushing forward against it with the heel of your hand, then fold it in half, give it a half turn, and push forward again (c). Repeat, turning in the same direction, for 15 minutes or until the dough is silky smooth and elastic.

4 Cut the dough into six pieces. Flatten one and wrap the rest separately in plastic wrap. Fold the flat piece in three (d) and pass it lengthways through the pasta machine, set at the widest opening (e). Repeat three or four times, folding the dough in thirds each time. Put the strips on a dishcloth and repeat with the other pieces.

5 Close the rollers by one notch and run all the strips through again, this time without folding them. Close the opening by another notch and repeat the procedure. Continue until the rollers are at the narrowest setting.

6 To make ribbons, cut the pasta into 12-inch strips and feed through the cutter of your choice (f). As the ribbons emerge, separate them carefully and spread out on dishcloths.

7 To dry the pasta, coil a few ribbons into a nest and leave to dry for 24 hours, making sure the nests do not touch. Store in an airtight container.

ricotta and mint tortelloni

Marcella Hazan is the doyenne of Italian cookery and one of the world's most respected food writers. In her delectable homemade tortelloni, silky, golden egg pasta is stuffed with ricotta cheese, mint, onion, and garlic. A bay leaf-scented tomato sauce provides the perfect complement. As Marcella says, "This has the briskest, lightest flavor of any stuffed pasta I know." The sauce can be cooked one or two days in advance, and reheated at a gentle simmer before tossing with the pasta. The tortelloni can be made as far ahead as early in the morning, if you are serving them for dinner.

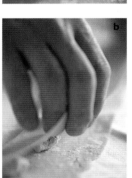

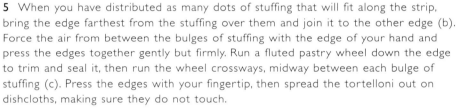

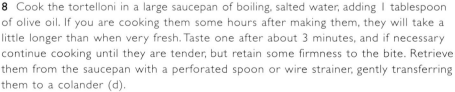

Makes about 36 tortelloni to serve 6 as an appetizer or 4 as a main course

Note: Pasta that is going to be stuffed should be soft and sticky, so the procedure given on page 113 must be adjusted as follows: take one piece of dough at a time through the entire thinning process and, before going on to the next piece, cut it and stuff it as described below.

1 Wrap the ricotta tightly in a layer of cheesecloth and drain for 30 minutes, as in the recipe for "yogurt cheese" on page 58. Place the ricotta in a bowl, add the nutmeg, mint, egg yolk, salt, and pepper, and mix well.

2 Put the butter and onion in a small skillet, turn the heat to medium, and cook the onion, stirring occasionally, until it turns a pale gold. Add the garlic and cook it, stirring frequently, until it is a shade of gold paler than the onion. Empty the contents of the pan into the ricotta mixture, stirring with a wooden spoon until uniformly mixed.

3 Following the instructions on page 113, make the dough with the eggs, flour, and the extra milk, then mix and knead it. Cut the dough into four pieces and take one piece through the entire rolling, folding, and thinning process, taking it down to the thinnest notch setting. Keep the rest of the dough covered in plastic wrap.

4 Lay a 6-inch wide, long strip of dough on a clean dishcloth. Dot with a row of cherry-size pellets of stuffing, setting them down 2¹/₂ inches apart and 1¹/₂ inches away from one long edge of the rectangle (a).

5 When you have distributed as many dots of stuffing that will fit along the strip, bring the edge farthest from the stuffing over them and join it to the other edge (b). Force the air from between the bulges of stuffing with the edge of your hand and press the edges together gently but firmly. Run a fluted pastry wheel down the edge to trim and seal it, then run the wheel crossways, midway between each bulge of stuffing (c). Press the edges with your fingertip, then spread the tortelloni out on dishcloths, making sure they do not touch.

6 Now repeat the entire thinning, stuffing, and cutting process with the remaining pieces of dough. The tortelloni can be cooked immediately or after several hours. If you are going to cook them later, turn them over every 15 minutes or so.

7 To make the sauce, put 2 tablespoons of butter and 1¹/₂ tablespoons of oil in a medium skillet over medium-high heat. Cook the onion, stirring, until it turns a medium gold. Add the bay leaves and cook for a few seconds, turning, then add the tomatoes, salt, and pepper. Cook at a steady but gentle simmer, stirring periodically, for about 15 to 20 minutes, until the fat floats free of the tomatoes.

8 Cook the tortelloni in a large saucepan of boiling, salted water, adding 1 tablespoon of olive oil. If you are cooking them some hours after making them, they will take a little longer than when very fresh. Taste one after about 3 minutes, and if necessary continue cooking until they are tender, but retain some firmness to the bite. Retrieve them from the saucepan with a perforated spoon or wire strainer, gently transferring them to a colander (d).

9 As soon as the tortelloni are done, place in a warm serving platter, and gently toss with 1 tablespoon of butter, the tomato sauce, and the grated Parmigiano-Reggiano. Serve at once.

Tools	Ingredients
cheesecloth	*For the stuffing:*
wooden spoon	1 cup whole milk ricotta
tall jug or bowl	1/8 tsp. freshly grated nutmeg
mixing bowl	4 tsp. chopped fresh mint leaves
nutmeg grater	1 egg yolk
small skillet	salt and freshly ground black pepper
several large dishcloths	1 tbsp. butter
hand-cranked pasta machine with 6-inch rollers	2 tbsp. finely chopped onion
	1/2 tsp. chopped garlic
	For the wrappers:
fluted pastry wheel	1 to 1 1/3 cups Italian '00' flour
utility knife	2 extra large eggs at room temperature
medium skillet	1 tbsp. milk
pasta pot	*For cooking the pasta and for the sauce:*
perforated spoon or wire strainer	2 tbsp. butter for the sauce, 1 tbsp. for tossing
colander	1 1/2 tbsp. extra-virgin olive oil for the sauce, 1 tbsp. for the pasta
Parmesan grater	1/2 small onion, finely chopped
	4 bay leaves
	12 oz. large, firm, ripe tomatoes, skinned, seeded, and chopped
	salt and freshly ground black pepper
	2/3 cup freshly grated Parmigiano-Reggiano

The smell and texture of fresh yeast, the rhythmic kneading, the perfect curve of risen dough, and the transformation to a fine-tasting, crusty loaf make breadmaking the most sensuous of culinary pleasures.

cake pans and trays

Cake baking is a precise skill requiring accuracy of weighing, temperature, and pan size. Pans of the same volume can have different dimensions—one may be wide and shallow, another narrow and deep. A mixture intended to cook quickly in a shallow pan will not cook properly in a pan that is too deep, and vice versa. A good recipe will specify the dimensions of the pan, not just the volume.

The most useful pans to have are a pair of round, shallow, 8-inch cake pans; a deep, 9- to 10-inch pan for fruitcake; a jelly-roll pan; and perhaps a 9-inch springform pan for easy release of molded cakes and desserts. One or two 12-cup trays are useful for muffins, cupcakes, and tarts, or dough left over from a large cake. Pans with a nonstick surface may not be foolproof, but they are worth having. For choice of materials, see "Bread-pan materials," page 117.

1 Joined small pans These differently shaped individual pans are joined together in a row for convenience. Choose from boats, rectangles, waisted ovals and many more. Once you have one sort, you'll want to collect more.

2 Foil and paper cupcake cases Useful for light mixes that cook very quickly, these can be placed on a cookie sheet or in the indented cups of a muffin pan. If they are left in place until ready to eat, paper cups prevent the cakes from drying out. Children love peeling them off.

3 English bun tray This 12-cup, nonstick tray is ideal for cupcakes and mini tarts and quiches. The ridged handles make the tray easier to grip when sliding it in and out of the oven.

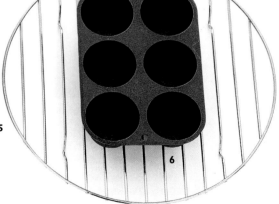

4 Yorkshire pudding tray Similar to the English bun tray, this one has four shallow, flat-bottomed cups for making single portions of Yorkshire pudding. The tray can also be used for baking small cakes and mini tarts and quiches.

5 Cooling racks An elevated wire rack speeds cooling of cakes by allowing steam to evaporate from all surfaces. A very fragile cake may be damaged by the wires, so cover the rack with a layer of waxed paper before placing the cake on it. The paper will absorb evaporating steam.

6 Popover/muffin pan Air circulates quickly between these individual cups pressed into a heavy, cast-iron sheet, promoting rapid rising and setting of dough. The flared, 1½-inch deep sides increase surface area, which encourages dough to rise and moisture to evaporate.

7 Angel food cake pan The tube allows heat to penetrate to the center of the cake and provides another surface for the mixture to cling to as it rises. The tube projects beyond the rim so when the pan is inverted to cool the cake, air can pass beneath it. Some pans have small feet on the rim for better balance when inverted.

8 Deep, round cake pans Dense Madeira cake or fruitcake mixtures need long baking, so should be baked in a deep, heavy-gauge pan to prevent scorching. These pans have a removable base and a reinforced, rolled rim that helps to maintain their shape.

9 Springform pan This is invaluable for fragile cakes that are hard to remove from the pan. When the clip is unbuckled, the sides of the pan move out from the base, leaving behind a perfectly formed cake. Made of heavy-gauge steel with a durable nonstick coating inside and out, this heavy-duty pan comes with an additional tube base embossed with swirling flutes. It is ideal for cheesecake.

10 Jelly-roll pan Extremely shallow, this rectangular pan is specially designed for cooking the thin layer of cake needed for a jelly roll. It is made from heavy-gauge tinned steel, which conducts heat quickly and evenly, and will not warp or twist.

11 Shallow cake pan This is used for quickly cooked mixtures such as round cake layers. It is best to buy a pair. Although it has a nonstick surface, it still needs to be greased.

12 Madeleine tray The scallop-shaped, fluted indentations increase the area that is exposed to heat. This allows the batter to rise quickly in the middle and produce the characteristic madeleine shapes.

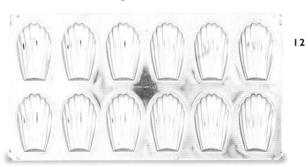

tart pans and pie plates

For a meltingly crisp, golden-brown pastry shell, use a fluted metal pan with a removable base. Some cooks use a bottomless metal ring set directly on a baking or cookie sheet. Though they are more attractive than metal dishes, tart dishes made of fluted porcelain absorb heat more slowly than metal and do not produce such a crisp crust.

The most useful diameters for tart pans are 9 and 10 inches. A high-sided tart pan comes in handy for making quiches. If you are partial to pies, deep and shallow ceramic pie dishes are worth buying, as is a metal pie plate for that spur-of-the-moment pie.

Rigid metal baking trays or sheets are essential for baking small pastry shapes, cookies, and hand-formed breads. They also provide porcelain dishes with a boost of heat from below, which helps to cook the base. It's worth buying two baking sheets so you can load one while the other is in the oven. Never put two in the oven simultaneously—the top one will prevent heat circulating over the lower, and you'll end up with unevenly cooked food. Buy the largest baking sheet your oven will accommodate, but allow at least 2 inches all around for air circulation.

1 Deep fluted tart pans The fluted sides of these metal pans almost double the surface area exposed to heat. This encourages the crust to set more quickly. Being deep, the sides make a particularly strong crust, which is useful for cream- or egg-based fillings containing solid pieces of food. The bases of these tins are removable (see 2).

2 Shallow fluted tart pans Perfect for glazed fruit tarts or shallow custard-filled tarts, these pans are available in sizes ranging from 4¹/₂ to 13 inches. As with the deep-fluted pans, the bases are removable for easy removal. Stand the pan on a jar and ease the outer ring down. You can leave the tart on the base when you transfer it to a serving plate.

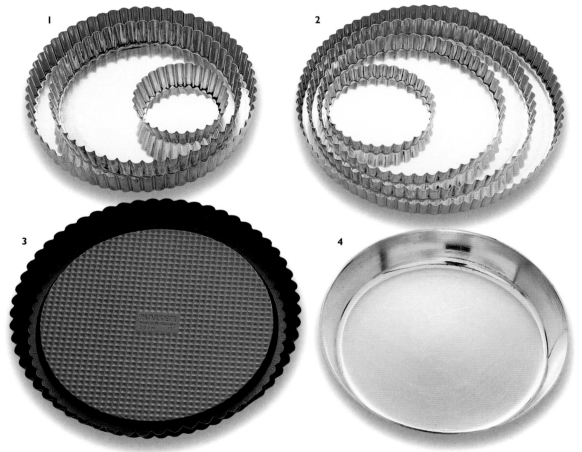

3 Nonstick sponge tart pan This warp-free pan with a raised center is used for baking those slightly old-fashioned whisked sponge cases that you load up with whipped cream and fruit. Once turned out, the base is left upside down, leaving a raised rim surrounding a circle for the filling. The base has a dimpled surface, which makes removal easier.

4 Tarte tatin pan Made of copper lined with stainless steel, this elegant pan is ideal for baking the upside-down apple cake known as "tarte tatin," because copper quickly conducts the high heat necessary for caramelizing syrupy juices. A wide base and shallow sides provide a large surface area, which allows the tart to cook evenly through to the center.

5 Deep pie dish This is one of those impeccably designed dishes that get handed down from generation to generation. It is made of thick, glazed ceramic, which allows steady heat to penetrate the center of the pie without burning the crust. The wide, flat rim supports the top layer of pastry and gives a generous seal, while the gently rounded interior makes serving and cleaning easier.

6 Pie bird The purpose of this porcelain bird is to support the top crust and vent the steam that would otherwise make the crust soggy. The slightly arced base allows steam to travel upward and out through the beak. Make sure the beak is wide open. You can also buy special funnels that serve the same purpose.

7 Shallow pie dish Like the deep dish (5), this classic piece of bakeware is made of thick, glazed ceramic with a flat rim for sealing double-crust pies. The round, shallow shape makes it a versatile dish—it can double up as a gratin dish and is elegant enough to be used as a serving bowl for vegetables, salad, or fruit.

8 Pie plates These lovely traditional tinned-steel plates are for baking shallow, double-crust pies or open tarts—the kind your grandmother used to make. They are available in a range of sizes, from a single serving to a family-sized 12 inches.

9 Nonstick pie plate with insert This pie plate is supplied with a useful perforated insert that can be used on its own instead of baking "beans" (see page 126) when baking an unfilled pastry case.

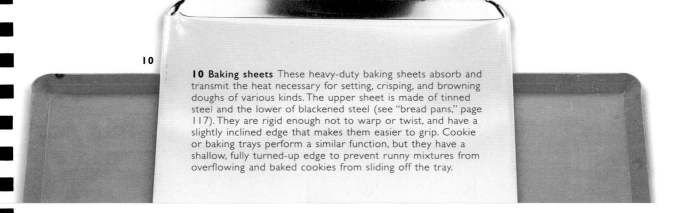

10 Baking sheets These heavy-duty baking sheets absorb and transmit the heat necessary for setting, crisping, and browning doughs of various kinds. The upper sheet is made of tinned steel and the lower of blackened steel (see "bread pans," page 117). They are rigid enough not to warp or twist, and have a slightly inclined edge that makes them easier to grip. Cookie or baking trays perform a similar function, but they have a shallow, fully turned-up edge to prevent runny mixtures from overflowing and baked cookies from sliding off the tray.

leek and peppercorn tart

A mouthwatering supper-time treat, this tart is made with rich piecrust dough. For maximum crispness, the pastry is rolled as thinly as possible and baked directly on a baking sheet at a high temperature. The leeks must be small and thinly sliced so they cook through. They will be tender but still crisp. The smoky flavor of green peppercorns is delicious with leeks and cheese.

Serves 4 to 6 as a light meal

Tools	Ingredients
flour sifter or sieve	1²/₃ cups plain unbleached flour
mixing bowl	¹/₄ tsp. each salt and sugar
utility knife	5 oz. butter
pastry blender	3 tbsp. iced water
coarse grater	3¹/₂ oz. cheddar cheese
mortar and pestle	3¹/₂ oz. mozzarella cheese
cook's knife	1¹/₂ tsp. dried green peppercorns
utility knife	salt
rolling pin	3 small leeks, weighing about 9 oz.
baking sheet	in total
small flat whisk	1³/₄ oz. pancetta
pastry brush	salt
	2 tsp. fresh thyme leaves
	beaten egg yolk, to glaze

1 Sift the flour, salt, and sugar into a bowl. Using a pastry blender if you wish, work in half the butter until the mixture resembles coarse crumbs (a). Briefly work in the remaining butter, leaving it slightly unevenly mixed. Lightly stir in the water to form a soft dough. Wrap in plastic wrap and chill for 1 hour.

2 Grate the cheeses, using the coarse blade of a grater. Crush the peppercorns with a mortar and pestle. Trim the leeks and slice in half lengthways, then crossways into 3/4-inch slices. You'll need about 1¹/₂ cups of prepared leek. Cut the pancetta into bite-size pieces.

3 Heat the oven to 475°F. Roll out the dough on a floured surface as thinly as possible to form a 12¹/₂-inch square (b). Carefully drape the dough over a rolling pin and place on a baking sheet (c). Trim the edges neatly.

4 Leaving a 3/4-inch border all around, scatter the cheeses evenly over the dough. Sprinkle with the peppercorns and a little salt to taste, then add the leeks, spreading them out evenly. Sprinkle with the pancetta and thyme.

5 Fold up the edges of the pastry to slightly enclose the filling, folding the corners to a pleat. Brush the edges with the egg yolk.

6 Bake for 20 minutes until the pastry is golden and the leeks look slightly charred. Serve hot or warm.

pastry paraphernalia

Making dough is a multistage process. You will need tools for blending, rolling, cutting, crimping, brushing, and scraping. Though much of this work can be done with your hands, using these tools makes life easier and gives a neater result.

A rolling pin is a must. Dough can be rolled with a broom handle or milk bottle, but neither are the ideal texture, length, or diameter. Rolling pins should be smooth to the touch, and longer than the area covered by the dough once it is rolled out. Metal rolling pins are cooler than wooden ones, but because wood is a poor conductor of heat, a wooden pin is pretty cool, too. The pin should be heavy enough to do its job without needing undue pressure from you. Though they can make pins more comfortable to use, handles reduce the width of the rolling surface or result in an unnecessarily long pin, which may be difficult to store.

1 Dough scraper Originally used for measuring and dividing dough into equal pieces, this traditional tool is now more often used as a scraper, though it still comes in handy for checking your dough is the right size.

2 Pastry wheel A fluted wheel gives a zigzag edge to lattice strips, pasta ribbons, and ravioli squares. The safety guard prevents your finger slipping onto the wheel.

3 Lattice cutter This ingenious tool saves the work of hand-weaving a lattice topping for a pie. Toothed wheels produce a series of broken lines as you roll the cutter over the dough. Gently lift and stretch the dough to open out the lattice.

4 Pastry blender A blender is useful for working fat into flour if your fingertips aren't up to it.

5 Flexible metal spatula Use this tool for evenly spreading and smoothing the surface of soft mixtures and toppings. Wetting the blade helps prevent sticking.

6 Natural bristle pastry brushes Bristles reach into crevices and coat surfaces evenly. These brushes are indispensable for anointing dough, dusting flour, or greasing pans. Wash and dry them after use.

Cutters
7 This double-ringed doughnut cutter prevents the off-center holes that may occur when using two separate cutters.
8 This covetable professional set includes cutters of every conceivable size. Use them to cut circles not only from dough, but also from firm fleshed vegetables, pineapple, aspic, and hard-boiled eggs. A rolled top edge maintains their shape.
9 More homely is this set of three crinkle cutters. Make sure you wash and dry them carefully after use to avoid rusting.

11 Wooden rolling pin This 15¼-inch professional pin sacrifices no rolling surface to handles.

10 Marble pastry board Cool, smooth marble is the ideal surface on which to roll dough. It needs very little flouring to prevent sticking.

12 Aluminum baking "beans" These small metal weights help to prevent blistering and shrinking in the first stage of baking a pastry case. Spread them thickly over the base of a foil-lined dough sheet, and remove them with the foil once the pastry has set.

molding
and
shaping

taking shape

Molded foods such as mousses, custards, and gelatin desserts seem to hark back to a more leisurely era when there was time for the setting and chilling these dishes need. Whether sweet or savory, such foods are by their very nature soft and delicate, and perhaps have been somewhat ousted from modern cooking with its insistence on speedy chargrilling and stir-frying, and bold, assertive flavors.

Despite changing trends, molds do have a place in today's kitchens, even if for only a simple concoction such as a child's birthday dessert. And let's not forget the most basic of modern molds—the ice-cube tray. Molds may either be decorative or utilitarian, tall or shallow, patterned or plain. They are often made of metals such as aluminum or copper, because these react very quickly to heat or cold; porcelain or glass is used where heat or cold needs to be retained. Confectionery molds are made of tinned steel, plastic, or rubber. Molds are often made in the shape of a fish or fruit to indicate the nature of the dish.

Mixtures for tall or ornate molds need to be more firmly set than for shallow ones, as they are more likely to collapse or leave part of their contents trapped in an intricate crevice. The smoother and shallower the mold, the easier it is to turn out.

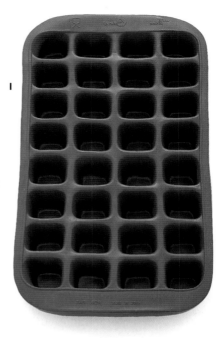

1 Giant ice-cube tray This brilliant ice-cube tray is flexible so you can remove cubes individually, and is supplied with a metal tray so it stays flat in the freezer.

2 Fish mold Ornate and versatile, this mold is equally suitable for a grown-up fish mousse or a bright orange childrens' gelatin dessert.

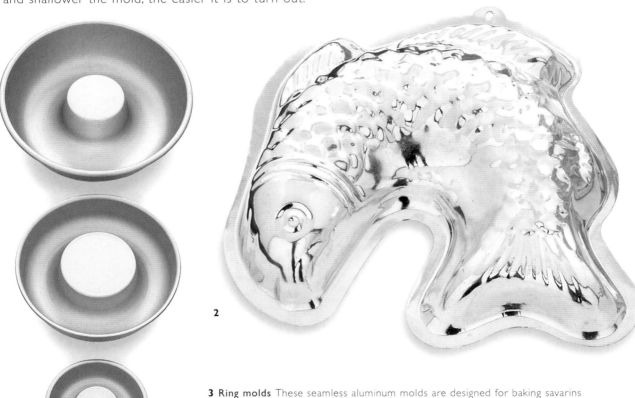

3 Ring molds These seamless aluminum molds are designed for baking savarins and babas—rich, yeasted cakes that are drenched in syrup or rum after cooking. The cake remains upside down after removal from the mold, and the depression in the center is piled high with whipped cream and/or fruit. A wide, shallow trough and a thick central tube allow maximum exposure to heat, so the mixture cooks quickly as it rises. Ring molds can also be used for mousses, custards, or rice.

4 Ice-cream bombe mold This smooth, spherical mold has a tightly fitting lid to prevent ice crystals forming during storage.

5 Charlotte mold To make a charlotte, this bucket-shaped aluminum mold is lined with buttered bread or ladyfingers and then filled with a fruit purée or mousse. The outwardly sloping sides make it easier to line and also allow it to be lifted free of its contents once inverted. Charlottes may be served uncooked and chilled, or baked in the oven and served hot—hence the mold's two heart-shaped handles. Either way, aluminum is an excellent conductor, speeding the penetration of heat or cold as appropriate.

6 Dariole molds These small, simple aluminum molds are good conductors of heat or cold. Use them for making tiny rum babas (but fill only halfway and allow the dough to rise before baking), crème caramels, timbales, and small steamed puddings.

7 Heart mold A tool for romantic cooks, this mold is ideal for sweet or savory dishes to celebrate Valentine's Day or anniversaries.

8 Gelatin dessert/blancmange molds These aluminum molds are embossed with simple patterns well suited to a gelatin dessert or blancmange. Make sure the top of the unfilled mold is level so that when inverted it does not wobble while the contents are setting.

presses and extruders

Some foods depend on special shaping—piped cake frosting, for example. Other foods, such as burgers or shortbread, simply look more appetizing if they are neatly formed or have a motif stamped on them.

These tools compress mixtures into a flat shape, sometimes embossing or sealing it in the process; otherwise they force the mixture through a tip or a specially shaped cutter. None of the tools are essential, unless you regularly frost cakes, but they are fun to use and do not cost the earth.

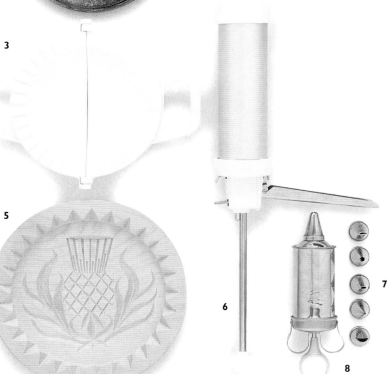

1 Burger press This cast-aluminum, cow-embossed, hinged press produces a compact, perfectly round burger. The press eliminates the air pockets that cause burgers to crack when turned.

2 Tortilla press As you pull down the handle of this ingenious press, two cast-aluminum hinged disks uniformly flatten a small ball of masa harina dough into a paper-thin tortilla.

3 Turnover press Making meat, fruit, or vegetable turnovers is easy with this hinged, semi-circular, plastic press, which simultaneously molds, crimps, and seals the pastry.

4 Pastry bags Pastry bags are used in conjunction with a decorating tube for piping semifluid mixtures that hold their shape. The bags are soft and pliable, and respond to the slightest pressure, so may require patience at first. These professional-quality bags are made of waterproof nylon and have a loop for hanging them up to dry.

7 Decorating tips Used with a pastry bag or syringe, these conical tips shape the mixtures that are forced through them. Tubes are made of metal, nylon, or plastic, and come in a wide range of sizes and shapes. Those with well-defined, sharp edges produce the most clean-cut designs. Use them for writing or for piping decorative shapes such as stars, rosettes, ribbons, or shells.

8 Frosting syringe Frosting is forced through the cylinder and tube by a plunger attached to a central shaft that passes through the lid. To operate the plunger, put your thumb through the central loop, hook your forefinger and middle finger through the loops on the lid, and press down.

5 Shortbread mold Beautifully and precisely carved, this handmade sycamore mold embosses a traditional thistle design on top of shortbread. Sycamore is a dense wood that is particularly suitable for carving intricate designs and producing a crisp imprint.

6 Cookie press There is no easier way to make cookies than with this sturdy aluminum press. A plunger forces dough through a decorative cutter, producing flawless cookies of various shapes. The gun is supplied with tips for piping fillings and decorations.

measuring

weight and volume

It was not until relatively recently that recipes began to specify exact amounts of ingredients. In the past, it was a matter of taking "some" of one ingredient, throwing in a handful of this and a pinch of that, and heating "until cooked." Nowadays, however, we go to the other extreme and probably over-specify. To complicate matters, some cookbooks specify two, sometimes even three, measuring systems: American, imperial, and metric.

American recipes specify the majority of ingredients by mass or volume, even though measuring by weight is more accurate and in some cases easier. For example, how do you measure a cup of tomatoes? Or a cup of something that does not easily fit into the shape of a measuring cup? Recipes from other countries specify solid or dry ingredients by weight, and liquid ingredients by volume. Small amount of dry ingredients are also measured by volume, that is in teaspoons or tablespoons.

Measuring equipment is not expensive, so it is worth investing in a set of scales and measuring jugs marked in ounces and pounds and metric measurements, particularly if you use recipes from different countries. You can then use either of the two systems; they are not necessarily interchangeable, because one set of measurements may have been rounded up or down to make a neat and tidy conversion rather than an exact one.

It is also worth buying several sets of measuring spoons, if only to save having to wash a single spoon each time you measure sticky or greasy ingredients.

When buying scales, the choice is between balance, electronic, and spring scales—each has its advantages and disadvantages. Balance scales look great, but are fiddly to use. The weights are sold separately, and you will need to buy two sets if you use both metric and imperial measurements. Electronic scales are the most accurate type, but you will need to keep replacing the batteries. Spring scales are easy to use, but need to be well built—once the spring breaks they are useless.

When choosing measuring jugs, remember that a more accurate measurement can be obtained from a tall, narrow jug than from a wide one. A narrow shape causes the contents to rise higher up the jug, so there is a greater distance between the calibrations printed on the side. The wider the space between each increment, the easier it is to see when the contents reach a particular level. Clear jugs are more useful than opaque ones, as they allow you to see the contents at eye level.

1 Balance scales Made to a traditional design, these attractive scales work by force of gravity: when the ingredients in the pan weigh the same as the metal weights on the platform, the beam is horizontal. Balance scales are accurate and built to last, but they are not quite as easy to use as either spring or electronic scales. They are also somewhat unwieldy, so are best kept on the countertop for convenience.

2 Electronic scales Meticulously accurate, these state-of-the-art scales are good-looking enough to grace the most design-conscious kitchen. The one slight drawback of this model is that the control switch for changing the readout from imperial to metric is under the base—other models have a more convenient button on top.

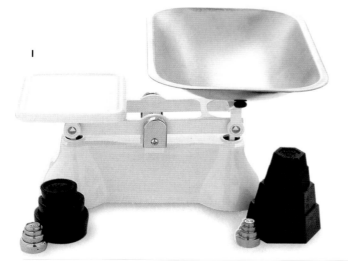

Measuring jugs

3 Invaluable in the kitchen, these tall plastic jugs can be used for measuring and pouring anything from a beaten egg to a large volume of stock. Very durable, they will withstand boiling liquids, and will not break if dropped. They are available in 2-cup, 1-quart, and 2-quart sizes.

4 This wide, 2-quart plastic jug can double up as a mixing bowl. It is especially useful for ingredients that need to be whisked, then poured in measured amounts—crêpe batter, for example.

5 A small Pyrex jug is useful for transferring hot soup or stock from one container to another. It is heatproof, easy to keep clean, and will not absorb grease or smells.

6 Dry measuring beaker
The inside of this classic aluminum beaker is printed with different scales showing the equivalent volume of a particular weight of various dry ingredients. It also shows American cups and pints, English cups, pints, and gills, as well as milliliters. The outside of the beaker is printed with metric/imperial conversions. Cheap, cheerful, and extremely useful.

7 European measuring cups
These charming liquid measuring cups are made of aluminum and have finger-friendly handles. They hold 50ml, 100ml, and 250ml.

9 British measuring spoons
Sensibly designed, these plastic spoons are narrow enough to reach inside spice jars. This comprehensive set includes the elusive 1/8 teaspoon and 1/2 tablespoon. It is worth buying at least three sets.

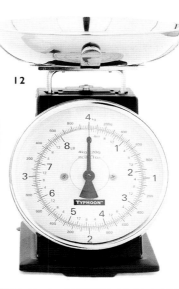

8 American measuring cups
These stylish stainless-steel cups are used for measuring liquids. The top measurement is printed just below the rim of the cup so the liquid does not overflow. (Dry measuring cups are filled to overflowing and then leveled off with a knife.) They hold 1/4, 1/3, 1/2, and 1 cup.

10 American measuring spoons
Made of heavy-gauge stainless steel, these measuring spoons are made to last. Buy several.

11 Diet scales A must for calorie counters, these scales accurately weigh very small portions of food, showing clearly whether or not that morsel of chocolate weighs 1/8 ounce or 1/4 ounce.

12 Spring scales Good looking and practical, these stainless-steel scales weigh up to 9 pounds of ingredients—about 1 pound more than most kitchen scales. The dial is clearly printed with metric and imperial measurements, and large enough to read 20-gram or 1-ounce calibrations with ease.

temperature and time

Degrees and minutes matter. A few seconds can turn toasted almonds into blackened fragments; a few degrees can dry out a moist braise. Whatever the dish, it is always worth checking the oven temperature with a thermometer before starting to cook. Thermostats are notoriously inaccurate so you may find the actual temperature differs from the one you have set.

Liquid-in-glass thermometers (with a graduated glass tube) are more accurate than spring-loaded ones (with a pointer). If you do decide to buy a spring-loaded thermometer, check that it is robustly made, as the spring is easily damaged.

Thermometers are also essential for food safety. Some foods, such as pork, chicken, and microwaved meals, must reach a specific internal temperature to destroy harmful bacteria. A meat thermometer and a microwave thermometer are invaluable for checking this. Refrigerators and freezers need to be kept below specific temperatures to slow the growth of harmful organisms. As neither appliance will necessarily maintain the correct temperature, a refrigerator/freezer thermometer is worthwhile.

A timer with a loud ring is invaluable for reminding forgetful cooks that food needs checking or removing from the oven or stovetop. A timer is also invaluable if you are cooking several dishes at once, or if you have the type of oven that does not transmit smells to warn you that food is burning.

1 Candy/fat thermometer This well-made thermometer is designed for confectionery and for deep-fat frying. The probe is immersed in boiling liquid and held in place by a spring clip attached to the side of the pan. The thermometer has a movable red clip attached to the rim to make it easier to see if the pointer has reached the correct position.

2 Meat thermometer Though your senses will usually tell you when meat is cooked, a thermometer is useful for moments of doubt. Insert the probe so the tip is close to the center of the meat. The meat is ready when the pointer moves to the appropriate wording (not shown). Like the candy/fat thermometer, it has a movable clip.

3 Spring-loaded oven thermometer As the oven heats up, a metal spring expands and moves the pointer. This one is sturdily made and hangs or stands in the oven. It has a wide base to prevent it from slipping between the racks.

4 Refrigerator/freezer thermometer This well-designed thermometer indicates the optimum range of temperatures at which refrigerators and freezers safely operate.

5 Digital probe thermometer A digital readout and a fold-away probe are two useful features of this thermometer. It operates through an impressive range of temperatures— from minus 57.8°F to 392°F.

6 Microwave thermometer When defrosting food or cooking in a microwave oven, it is vital that the food reaches a safe temperature through to the center. This plastic thermometer is especially designed so that it can be inserted deep into the food. The metal pin supplied with it is used to penetrate frozen food before the thermometer is inserted.

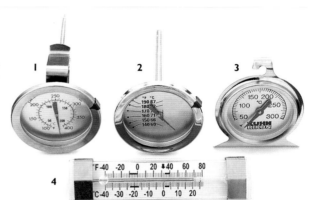

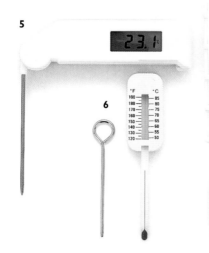

7 Water/chocolate thermometer The scale on this thermometer goes up to 140°F, which is the optimum temperature for tempering chocolate— the process of heating and cooling that stabilizes emulsified fats. The thermometer is also useful for checking the temperature of water intended to simmer rather than boil—in a bain marie, for instance. It is protected by a removable nylon cage.

8 Sugar/jam thermometer Made to a traditional design, this thermometer is indispensable when making jams and confectionery. It indicates the point at which sterilization takes place, and the stages in jam boiling and syrup making (wording not shown).

9 Spirit oven thermometer This is the most accurate and reliable type of oven thermometer. It shows heating zones as well as temperature (wording not shown), has a clear spirit tube, and hangs or stands in the oven.

10 Rotary electronic timer This easily operated electronic timer is set by rotating the dial forward or backward to display the chosen time, and pressing the button. It counts upward or downward, has an insistent ring, and will clip, hang, stand, or magnetize according to your needs.

11 Clockwork timer With its resounding ring, this compact 60-minute timer is easily heard. It is also easy to use. It hangs as a magnet or by a convenient hook, and if you are venturing far from the kitchen, you can keep it on a string around your neck.

12 Hourglass timer Designed by Robert Welch, this is a classic, gravity-based timer for those who like their eggs cooked for exactly three minutes. An enameled cast-iron frame protects the glass.

10

11

12

Egg boiling times

For best results, place an egg in cold water and begin timing the instant the water starts to boil.

At one minute the white starts to set, but the yolk is barely heated. A Caesar's salad dressing uses an egg boiled for one minute.

At three minutes the white is lightly set and creamy; the yolk is hot but still runny. French chefs call this an "oeuf mollet." This is the classic breakfast egg in which to dip your toast, or for serving in a bed of spinach, as in eggs Florentine.

At six minutes the white and yolk are set, but the center of the yolk is very slightly creamy. Halved or quartered, these eggs make attractive garnishes. Halved eggs can be stuffed—remove the yolk, mix with your chosen seasoning, and pile back in the egg.

At ten minutes the whites and yolk are tough, with a thin, dark line between the two. The whites and yolks can be rubbed through a sieve separately for use as a garnish—for veal schnitzels or Jewish chopped liver, for instance.

Jams and jellies Jams and fruit jellies set at just below 221°F, when the dissolved sugar interacts with the acid and natural fruit pectin. To check if it has set, spoon a sample of the freshly cooked jam or jelly onto a chilled saucer and after a couple of minutes push it with your fingertip—if a skin forms, it is set.

Sugar syrup Boiling sugar and water to make a syrup causes the water to evaporate, concentrating the density of the syrup. This is useful for making confectionery and recipes that need different strengths of syrup. If you drop small amounts of hot syrup into iced water they form either a soft ball (at 239 to 244°F) or a hard ball (at 248 to 252°F).

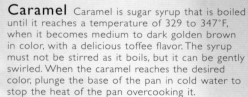
Caramel Caramel is sugar syrup that is boiled until it reaches a temperature of 329 to 347°F, when it becomes medium to dark golden brown in color, with a delicious toffee flavor. The syrup must not be stirred as it boils, but it can be gently swirled. When the caramel reaches the desired color, plunge the base of the pan in cold water to stop the heat of the pan overcooking it.

storing food

covering up

All food should be covered, regardless of where you store it. Leaving food exposed not only allows molds and bacteria to get to work (and they do so even in the refrigerator), but also allows air, heat, and light to destroy valuable nutrients. So, for the sake of your health, it is important to invest in suitable containers and get in the habit of using them.

Top of the list should be a collection of airtight plastic boxes. Buy several sizes and shapes: deep, shallow, large, and small, remembering that square and rectangular boxes make more efficient use of available space than round ones. Buy self-adhesive labels so you can identify the contents easily.

Equally invaluable are foil and plastic wrap. Both are handy for wrapping things tightly or covering bowls. Plastic bags are essential for sandwiches and for anything that needs gathering together in a flexible container.

Glass storage jars look attractive, but they are not airtight, nor do they protect the contents from light. They are suitable only for nonperishables such as dried pasta and legumes. Spices and dried herbs should be kept in airtight containers away from light. Nuts and wholewheat flour need airtight containers, too, as they contain fats that eventually become rancid if exposed to air. They also need protection from heat, so don't store these items in a cupboard close to a heating pipe or an under-unit strip light.

1

1 Plastic storage bags These are a household essential for wrapping sandwiches or for preventing moisture loss from fruit and vegetables while stored in the refrigerator. Heavy-gauge bags can be used for storing food in the freezer.

2 Aluminum foil
Foil is used not only to protect food and pans during cooking, but also to exclude air during storage. Being flexible, it can be wrapped tightly around any awkwardly shaped items, such as a cooked chicken. Foil also keeps sandwiches fresh and prevents loose or chunky fillings from escaping. Unlike plastic wrap, it does not cause cheese to sweat. Buy the heaviest grade possible—though cheaper, thin foil tears easily so what you save in money you waste in damaged foil.

2

3

4

4 Foil dishes Made from heavyweight aluminum foil, these are versatile containers in which to freeze, transport, or reheat food. A flexible rim folds over a flat cardboard lid, which rests on the flattened edge. Though the foil containers are reusable, the perishable lids limit their useful life.

5 Foil bag Strong and flexible, this plastic-lined foil bag is ideal for freezing liquids such as soup.

5

3 Plastic wrap Use plastic wrap for tightly wrapping food or for covering bowls. Ordinary plastic wrap should never be used in direct contact with very fatty foods, such as butter, high fat cheeses (e.g. cheddar), or food in an oily medium (e.g. tuna in oil), as harmful substances in the plastic can migrate into the food. When covering bowls for use in a microwave, do not let plastic wrap come in direct contact with the food unless the words "Safe for use in the microwave" are printed on the packaging.

6 Cheese dome Cheese needs a cool temperature and circulating air during storage. This attractive glass dome keeps cheese fresh and moist while it is at room temperature. The wooden base has a channel around the edge to keep the dome in place.

Mesh covers
7 In pre-refrigeration days, an oval wire-mesh cover was used to protect meat from dust and flies. It allowed air to circulate around the meat, keeping it fresher than a close-fitting wrapping. Nowadays you might use it for refrigerated meat that you are allowing to come to room temperature before barbecuing.
8 This square nylon food umbrella can be used as temporary protection for any food that will fit under it. It can be folded flat when not in use.

9 Condiment jars These attractive jars are made of glazed stoneware and are traditionally used for potted goose and pork. Though not airtight, they do exclude light. They are best used for anything submerged in a protective liquid—such as olives in oil, or pickles in brine—and for dripping and lard. Straight sides, a wide neck, and an easily removable lid make them easy to fill and reach into.

10 Garlic pot Garlic bulbs need access to air to prevent mold, and protection from light to stop premature sprouting. This pot provides both.

11 Preserving jar Certain foods will keep for months if they are vacuum packed in a sterilized container and submerged in a medium suitable for keeping bacteria at bay—acid, brine, or oil, for example. This classic glass preserving jar fits the bill. It can be sterilized in the oven and has a rubber gasket and wire clip to seal the lid. The neck is wide enough for easy filling.

12 Butter dish A deep container is useful for protecting a block of butter when not in the refrigerator. This porcelain butter dish is good-looking enough to be brought to the table.

13 Stainless-steel container This airtight container has a well-fitting lid and is useful for storing cakes, cookies, or homemade muesli. It is smart enough to keep on the countertop.

14 Food boxes These versatile plastic boxes are suitable for the freezer, refrigerator, cupboard, for picnics and packed lunches, and for reheating food in the microwave. Tightly fitting indented lids seal in smells, exclude air, and facilitate easy stacking. When not in use, smaller boxes nest in larger ones, saving on storage space. They are available with different colored lids for easy identification.

15 Enameled bread bin This traditional bread bin is made of sturdy enameled steel. It is not airtight as bread needs to be ventilated but kept dry. Remove all crumbs every few days to prevent mold. Wash and dry well every week or two.

16 Enameled container Containers like these are not airtight, but they are suitable for storing items that are quickly used up and need to be easily accessible, such as sugar, tea, and coffee.

sources

The following list will help you find many of the items featured in this book. Wherever possible we have given the names of manufacturers so you can contact them to find suppliers in your area (see "manufacturers and distributors"). Alternatively, you can contact the retailers listed on pages 141 to 142. If tools are omitted from the list it is because the manufacturer is unknown. However, you can find these or similar items at good kitchenware stores.

Page
10 1 bread knife, 2 cook's knife, 3 utility knife, 4 tomato/sandwich knife, 5 paring knife, and 6 vegetable knife by Zwilling J.A. Henckels; 7 knife block by Victorinox
11 8 V-shaped sharpener by Taylor's Eye Witness; 10 sharpening steel by Global
12 2 carving knife and fork by Le Creuset Sabatier
13 3 ham/smoked salmon slicer by Lion Sabatieri; 4 freezer knife by Gustav Emil Ern; 5 filleting knife and 6 boning knife by Zwilling J.A. Henckels; 9 grapefruit knife by Rösle; 10 oyster knife by Wüsthof Trident; 11 cleaver by Global; 12 and 13 Japanese knives by Yoshikin
16 3 Y-shaped peeler by Good Grips; 4 cannelle knife by Rösle; 6 pizza wheel by Rösle; 7 cheese plane by Wüsthof Trident; 8 plastic bean slicer by Krisk; 9 metal bean slicer by Porkert
17 11 black mandoline by Matfer; 15 french-fry cutter by Zyliss; 17 fish scaler by Fox Run
24 4 apple corer and 5 courgette corers by Pedrini; 6 pineapple corer/slicer by Vacu Vin
25 10 kabob skewers, 11 small round skewers, and 12 potato baking spike by Rösle; 14 chrome can opener by Pedrini; 15 screwpull corkscrew by Screwpull® Le Creuset; 16 winged corkscrew by Pedrini; 17 lever-based corkscrew by Screwpull® Le Creuset
28 1 stand mixer by KitchenAid; 2 food processor by Magimix; 3 stick blender by Braun
29 4 blender by Waring; 5 juicer by Braun; 6 multipurpose kitchen machine by Bosch; 7 handheld mixer by Kenwood
32 1 ceramic spice mill by Trudeau; 2 Crushgrind® spice mill by T.&G. Woodware; 3 meat grinder by Porkert; 5 wooden salt and pepper mills by William Bounds
33 6 electric coffee grinder by Krups; 12 nutmeg mill by William Bounds
36 1 porcelain grater by Fox Run; 2 citrus grater by Sveico; 3 flat graters by Rösle; 4 box grater by Sveico; 5 Microplane® grater by Grace Manufacturing; 7 rotary grater by Fox Run
38 2 meat mallet/tenderizer by Fox Run; 3 garlic press by Bodum; 7 potato masher by Good Grips
39 8 cone nutcrackers by Kitchen Craft; 10 pincer nutcrackers by Pedrini; 13 lemon reamer by Good Grips
42 1 basic glass bowl by Bodum; 3 stainless-steel bowls by Rösle; 5 melamine bowl by T.&G. Woodware; 6 ceramic bowl by Mason Cash
43 6 wire mixing spoon by Rösle; 8 insulated ice-cream scoop by Fox Run
44 1 salad dressing ladle and 2 portioning ladle by Rösle; 4 Chinese wok ladle by Typhoon; 7 colored plastic spatula by Le Creuset
46 1 balloon whisk, 2 egg whisk, 3 twirl whisk, 4 spiral whisk, 5 jug whisk, and 6 flat whisk by Rösle
54 1 flour and sugar dredgers by George East; 2 drum sieve by T.&G. Woodware; 3 flour sifter by Ekco
55 5 and 6 bowl-shaped sieves by Rösle
56 1 cheesecloth by Ekco; 2 stainless-steel colander by Rösle; 4 enameled colander by George East
57 6 perforated spoon by Paul Mitton/H. Faith; 7 tea strainer and 8 conical strainer by Rösle; 12 wire shaker by SEFAMA; 13 salad spinner by Zyliss
64 1 nonstick aluminum saucepan by Berndes; 2 stainless-steel saucepans by Cuisinox
65 3 anodized aluminum saucepans by Calphalon; 4 anodized aluminum milk pan by Meyer
66 1 stockpot with pasta insert, Le Pentole pot by ICM; 2 pressure cooker by Kuhn Rikon; 3 double boiler, Le Pentole pan by ICM
67 6 slant-sided aluminium saucepan by Mermaid; 7 slant-sided anodized aluminium saucepan by Calphalon; 9 butter melter by Rösle
69 2 zabaglione pan and 3 sugar boiler by Mauviel; 4 saucier by All-Clad; 5 cheese-fondue pot by Emile Henry
72 1 drip-filter coffeemaker by Krups; 2 percolator by Cuisinart; 4 traditional espresso maker by Pezzetti; 6 plunger coffeemaker by Fox Run
73 1 whistling kettle by Alessi; 2 cordless kettle by Bodum; 3 traditional kettle by Le Creuset; 5 glass teapot/tea press by Bodum
74 1 couscousier by LI International; 2 three-piece

steamer by Cuisinox; 3 bamboo steamers by Typhoon
75 6 plum-pudding steamer and 7 expandable steamer basket by Fox Run; 11 "universal" steamer insert by Cuisinox
80 2 wok by Typhoon; 4 stainless-steel sauté pan, Le Pentole pan by ICM
81 5 splatter screen by Ekco; 6 hard-anodized aluminium stir-fry pan by Meyer; 7 steel omelette pan by Rösle; 8 hard-anodized aluminum chef's pan by Meyer
82 1 crêpe pan and 2 oval pan by Matfer; 3 fajita pan by Calphalon; 4 blini pan by Matfer
83 5 Danish cake pan by Lodge; 7 paella pan by Meyer; 8 chestnut pan by Fox Run
86 3 potato nest fryers by Wirax; 4 electric deep-fryer by Magimix
89 3 kitchen torch by Kitchen Craft; 4 reversible grill by Lodge
90 5 flat stovetop grill by Typhoon; 8 waffle iron by SEFAMA
92 1 long-handled fork, turner, and tongs by Good Grips, basting brush by Fox Run; 2 oval portable barbecue by Lodge; 5 wire holders by Fox Run
93 6 pedestal barbecue by SAEY; 7 kettle barbecue by Weber-Stephen Products
96 2 wok turner by Meyer; 3 fish turner by Rösle; 5 scissor-action tongs by Fox Run; 6 angled turner by Rösle; 8 bamboo rice paddle and fork by Typhoon; 9 wire scoop and 10 turning fork by Rösle
98 4 lifting forks by George East
99 acrylic fat separator by Fox Run; 7 vertical chicken roaster by Fox Run;10 V-shaped roasting rack by Fox Run; 11 bulb baster by Ekco
102 1 braising pan by All-Clad; 2 Brittany pot and 3 tagine by Le Creuset; 4 French oven by All-Clad
103 5 nonstick casserole by SKK Küchen- und Gasgeräte; 6 enameled Dutch oven by Le Creuset; 7 cast-iron Dutch oven and 8 brushed stainless-steel casserole by Hackman; 9 polished stainless-steel casserole by Taylor's Eye Witness
104 1 bean pot/fait-tout by Emile Henry; 2 marmite by Gres et Poteries de Digoin; 3 oval terrine by Emile Henry; 5 round terracotta pot by Gres et Poteries de Digoin
108 1 rectangular ceramic gratin dishes and 2 oval ceramic gratin dishes by Emile Henry; 3 porcelain, soufflé dishes by Apilco; 4 enameled cast-iron egg dish and 5 enameled cast-iron baking dish by Le Creuset; 6 porcelain ramekins, 7 porcelain oval gratin dishes, and 8 porcelain chocolate pots by Apilco
109 9 earthenware potato baker by Gres et Poteries de Digoin; 10 glazed earthenware bowls by Mason Cash; 11 cast-iron rectangular terrine by Le Creuset
112 1 perforated pizza pan by George East; 3 pizza peel/paddle by Fox Run; 4 ravioli tray, 5 pasta machine by Imperia
117 1 brioche pan by Matfer; 3 nonstick French bread pan by Fox Run; 4 hinged pan by Le Creuset
120 1 joined small pans by Metalurgica; 2 foil and paper cupcake cases by Fox Run; 3 English bun tray and 4 Yorkshire pudding tray by Kaiser; 5 cooling racks by Wirax
121 8 deep, round cake pans by Tathams Tinware; 9 springform pan by Kaiser; 10 jelly-roll pan by Le Creuset; 11 shallow cake pan by Kaiser
122 1 deep fluted tart pans and 2 shallow fluted tart pans by Le Creuset; 3 nonstick sponge tart pan by Kaiser; 4 tarte tatin pan by Mauviel
123 5 deep pie dish by Mason Cash; 6 pie bird by ICTC; blackened steel baking sheet by Bourgeat
126 6 natural bristle pastry brushes by Kaiser; 7 double-ringed doughnut cutter, 9 crinkle cutters, and 10 marble pastry board by Fox Run; 12 aluminum baking "beans" by Matfer
128 1 giant ice-cube tray by Lékué Articulos Menaje; 3 ring molds by Bradford Metal Spinning Co.
129 1 charlotte mold by Le Creuset; 8 large gelatin dessert/blancmange mold by Metalurgica, small gelatin dessert/blancmange mold by Fox Run
130 3 turnover press by Fox Run; 4 pastry bags by Staines Catering Equipment; 7 Decorating tips and 8 frosting syringe by George East
132 2 electronic scales by Soehnle
133 3, 4 measuring jugs by Stewart; 5 Pyrex measuring jug by Ekco; 6 dry measuring beaker by George East; 11 diet scales by Fox Run; 12 spring scales by Typhoon
134 1 candy/fat and 2 meat thermometer by Fox Run; 3 spring-loaded oven thermometer by Kuhn Rikon; 6 microwave thermometer by George East; 7 water/chocolate thermometer by Matfer; 8 sugar/jam thermometer and 9 spirit oven thermometer by Brannan
135 12 hourglass timer by Robert Welch Designs
139 7 wire-mesh cover by Wirax; 8 nylon food umbrella by Fox Run; 10 condiment jars and 12 garlic pot by Renault; 12 butter dish by ICTC; 13 stainless-steel container by Rösle; 15 enameled bread bin and 16 enameled container by George East

manufacturers and distributors

This list should be used with the "sources" list to track down particular items featured in the book. Contact manufacturers for details about your nearest supplier. Where there is no U.S. office for a company we have given the distributor or importer, or the address of the main office abroad.

Alessi S.p.A.
Via Privata Allessi 6, 2282, Crusinallo (VB), Italy
011 (39) 032-386-8611
All-Clad Metalcrafters
424 Morganza Road, Canonsburg, PA 15317
1-800-255-2523, 724-745-8300
Apilco
U.S. importer:
Cuthbertson Imports Inc, 6 Hollyhock Road, Wilton, CT 06897
203-834-0506
Berndes
1200-G Westinghouse Boulevard, Charlotte, NC 29273
704-588-8090
Bodum, Inc.
2920 Wolff Street, Racine, WI 53404
414-633-6450
Robert Bosch Sales Corp.
2800 South 25th Avenue, Broadview, IL 6153
708-865-5200
Bourgeat
Les Abrets, 38490, Isère, France
011 (33) 476-321-444
Bradford Metal Spinning Co. Ltd.
Bradware Industrial Park, Leonard Street, Bingley, Yorkshire BD16 1DP, U.K.
011 (44) 1274-511911
S. Brannan & Sons Co. Ltd.
c/o The Ever Ready Thermometer Co. Inc., 228 Lackawanna Avenue, West Paterson, NJ 07424
973-812-7474
Braun
c/o The Gillette Group, Corporate Offices, Prudential Tower Building, Boston, MA 02199
617-742-17000
Calphalon Corporation
P.O. Box 583, Toledo, OH 43697.0583
419-666-8700
Cusinart
1 Cummings Point Road, Stamford, CT 06902
203-975-4600
Cuisinox
U.S. distributor: Lunt Silversmiths, 298 Federal Street, P.O. Box 1010, Greenfield, MA 01302-1010
413-774-2774
Ekco Housewares
1 Pyrex Place, P.O. Box 1555, Elmira, NY 14902-1555
607-377-8207
Emile Henry U.S.A.
204 Quigley Boulevard, New Castle, DE 19720
302-326-4800
Fox Run Craftsmen
1907 Stout Drive, P.O. Box 2727, Warminster, PA 18974
215-675-7700
George East (Housewares) Plc
29 High Street, West Wickham, Kent BR4 0LP, U.K.
011 (44) 208-777-0444
email info@george-east.com
Global
U.S. importer: Sointu U.S.A., Inc., 443 Greenwich Street, New York, NY 10013
212-219-8585
Good Grips
Oxo International Ltd., 75 9th Avenue, 5th Floor, New York, NY 10011
212-242-3333
Grace Manufacturing
U.S. and Canadian distributor: Grey Gourmet, Inc., 415 Merton Street, Toronto M4S 1B4, Canada
416-487-9232
Gres et Poteries de Digoin
U.S. importer: Mouli Manufacturing Corp., 1 Montgomery Street, Belleville, NJ 07109
973-751-6900
Gustav Emil Ern
c/o M.Gilbert (Greenford) Ltd., Gilbert House, 1 Warwick Place, Warwick Road, Borehamwood. Herts WD6 1UA, U.K.
011 (44) 208-731-3700
Hackman
Hackman Designor Oy Ab, Hämeentie 135, FIN-00560 Helsinki, Finland
011 (358) 0204-3911
ICM SpA
Via Don Minzoni 1, 25066 Lumezzane (Brescia), Italy
011 (39) 030-897-9011

ICTC
The Intercontinental Cooking & Tableware Co. Ltd.,
3 Caley Close, Sweet Briar Road, Norwich NR3
2BU, U.K.
011 (44) 1603-488019

Imperia Trading
Corso Moncenisio 107, 10057 S. Anbrogio di
Torino, Italy
011 (39) 011-956-1377

Kaiser Bakeware, Inc.
1200-G Westinghouse Boulevard, Charlotte,
NC 29273
704-588-8090

Kenwood
c/o Krups North America, Inc., 7 Reuten Drive,
Closter, NJ 07624
201-76-5500

KitchenAid
P.O. Box 218, St. Joseph, MI 49088
1-800-541-6390

Kitchen Craft®
Thomas Plant (Birmingham) Ltd., 93–99 Holloway
Head, Birmingham B1 1QS, U.K.
011 (44) 121-604-6000
email info@thomasplant.co.uk

Krisk
U.S. distributor: SCI Cuisine International, 740
Pancho Road, Camarillo, CA 93011
805-482-0791

Krups North America, Inc.
7 Reuten Drive, Closter, NJ 07624
201-767-5500

Kuhn Ricon Corp.
350 Bon Air Center, Greenbrae, CA 94904
1-800-662-5882

Le Creuset of America, Inc.
Low Country Industrial Park, 1 Bob Gifford
Boulevard, Highway 68, Early Branch, SC 29916
803-943-4308

Lékué®
Articulos Menaje, c/Cadaques, 29-08120-La Llagosta
(Barcelona), Spain
011 (34) 3-574-26-40

Li International Trading Co.
11F Block Q, Yuen Sat Building, 1-1B Nelson Street,
Kowloon, Hong Kong
011 (852) 2084-870405

Lion Sabatier
c/o Le Creuset of America, Inc., Low Country
Industrial Park, 1 Bob Gifford Boulevard, Highway
68, Early Branch, SC 29916
803-943-4308

Lodge Manufacturing Co.
6th Street at Railroad, P.O. Box 380, South
Pittsburg, TN 37380
423-837-7181

Magimix U.K. Ltd.
19 Bridge Street, Godalming, Surrey GU7 1HY, U.K.
011 (44) 1483-427411

Mason Cash & Co. Ltd.
Pool Street, Church Gresley, Swadlingcote,
Derbyshire DE11 8EQ, U.K.
011 (44) 1283-217521

Matfer
9–11 Rue du Tapis Vert, 93260 Les Lilas, France
011 (33) 1436-260040

Mauviel
U.S. importer: Harold Import, 140 Lehigh Avenue,
Lakewood, NJ 08701
908-367-2800

Mermaid®
Samuel Groves, P.O.Box 1452, Hockley, Birmingham
B18 5RG, U.K.
011 (44) 121-554-2001
email sales@samuelgroves.co.uk

Metalurgica
Rua Alto da Mina, Zona Industrial, 4440 Campo
(Valongo), Portugal
011 (351) 122-451-6989

Meyer
Meyer Plaza, Vallejo, San Francisco, CA 94590
707-551-2800

Moulinex
c/o Krups North America, Inc., 7 Reuten Drive,
Closter, NJ 07624
201-767-5500

Paul Mitton/H. Faith
Unit 7, Trident Way International Trading Estate,
Brent Road, Southall, Middlesex UP2 5LF, U.K.
011 (44) 208-574-1888

Pedrini U.S.A., Inc.
125 Cartwright Loop, Bayport, New York,
NY 11705
516-472-4501

Pezzetti
20038 Seregno, Milan, Italy

Porkert
c/o Pragotrade U.S.A., Inc., 33426 Liberty Parkway,
North Ridgeville, OH 44039
440-353-3857

Renault
U.S. importer: Bridge Kitchenware Corp., 214 East
52nd Street, New York, NY 10022
1-800-274-3435

Robert Welch Studio Shop
Lower High Street, Chipping Campden,
Gloucestershire GL55 6DU, U.K.
011 (44) 1386-840522

Rösle U.S.A. Corp.
204 Quigley Boulevard, New Castle, DE 19720
302-328-4801

SAEY
Industrielaan 4, B-9501 Kortrijk, Heule, Belgium
011 (32) 563-7-15-15

SEFAMA
246 Chemin des Pommieries, 69400 Villefranche sur
Saône, France
011 (33) 474-094020

SKK Küchen-und Gasgeräte GmbH
D-41751 Viersen, Nettetaler Strasse 172-180,
Germany
011 (49) 2153-89103

Soehnle
U.S. distributor: Frieling U.S.A., 1920 Center Park
Drive, Charlotte, NC 28217
704-329-5100

Staines Catering Equipment
Unit 7, Trident Way, International Trading Estate
Brent Road, Southall, Middlesex UB2 5LG, U.K.
011 (44) 208-574-2322

The Stewart Company
Stewart House, Waddon Marsh Way, Purley Way,
Croydon CR9 4HS, U.K.
011 (44) 208-686-2231

Sveico AB
S 33500 Gnosjo, Sweden
011 (46) 37-032-5005

Tathams Tinware
20 Forest Business Park, South Access Road,
Walthamstow, London E17 8BA, U.K.
011 (44) 208-520-5206
email tinware@tathams.co.uk

Taylor's Eye Witness
Harrison Fisher & Co. Ltd.., Milton St., Sheffield,
Lancs S3 7WJ, U.K.
011 (44) 114-272-4221

T.&G. Woodware
Unit 9A-10B, Old Mill Road, Portishead, Bristol
BS20 7BX, U.K.
011 (44) 1-275-841841
email tg.woodware@virgin.net

Trudeau
18 Sidney Circle, Kenilworth, NJ 07033-1051
908-964-6555

Typhoon Products
Adams House, Dickerage Lane, New Malden, Surrey
KT3 3SF, U.K.
011 (44) 208-942-9361
email info@typhooneurope.com

Vacu Vin U.S.A., Inc.
P.O. Box 5489, Novato, CA 94948-5489
415-382-1241

Victorinox
U.S. importers: Swiss Army Brand, Inc., 1 Research
Drive, Shelton, CT 06484
203-929-6391

Waring Products Division
283 Main Street, New Hartford, CT 06057
1-800-269-6640

Weber-Stephen Products Co.
200 East Daniles Road, Palatine, IL 60067-6266
847-705-8660

William Bounds
P.O. Box 1547, Torrance, CA 90505-0547
310-375-0505

William Levene Ltd.
c/o West 175 2203 Airport Way South, Suite 801,
Seattle, WA 98134
206-233-0750

Wirax Wirewares Ltd..
Warstock Road, Kings Heath, Birmingham
B14 4RW, U.K.
011 (44) 121-474-2212

Wüsthof Trident
Ed. Wüsthof Dreizackwerk, P.O. Box 10 13 84,
D-42648 Solingen, Germany
011 (49) 212-20-67-0

Yoshikin
U.S. importer: Sointu U.S.A., Inc., 443 Greenwich
Street, New York, NY 10013
212-219-8585

Zwilling J.A. Henckels AG
P.O. Box 100864, D-5650 Solingen, Germany
011 (49) 212-882-314

Zyliss Haushaltwaren AG
Industriezon Nord, Schachenweg 24, Ch-3250 Lyss,
Switzerland
011 (41) 32-384-3322

retailers

A Cook's Wares
211 37th Street, Beaver Falls, PA 15010
1-800-915-9788
www.cookswares.com
Bakeware, cutlery, small appliances, cookware,
utensils. (Demeyere, Henckels, Wüsthof, KitchenAid,
Cuisinart, Kuhn Rikon, All-Clad)

ABC Carpet & Home
888 Broadway, New York, NY 10003
212-473-3000
Outlet—1055 Bronx River Ave., Bronx, NY
718-842-8770
www.abchome.com
Cookware, bakeware, utensils, cutlery, textiles/linens,
small appliances, kitchen tools. (All-Clad, Le
Creuset, Oxo, Wüsthof, Emile Henry, Mauviel of
France, Chantal, Riess, Pedrini, Waring)

Bridge Kitchenware
214 East 52nd Street, New York, NY 10022
212-688-4220
www.bridgekitchenware.com
Specializing in imported tools and cookware for
professionals. (Ateco, Sitram, Paderno, Wüsthof
Cutlery and Chef's Cutlery) Catalogue and mail
order available.

Broadway Panhandler
477 Broome Street, New York, NY 10013
212-966-3434
www.broadwaypanhandler.com
Kitchenware for the professional and home chef.
Cookware, cutlery, bakeware, glassware, decorative
accessories, kitchen tools and small appliances.
(Le Creuset, KitchenAid, Rusthof, Cuisinart, Krups
and Bourgeat)

Fante's (2 locations in PA)
1006 South Ninth Street, South Philadelphia,
PA 19147
215-922-5557
In the Plaza at King of Prussia
Route 202 at Mall Boulevard, King of Prussia,
PA 19406
610-265-8288
1-800-443-2683
www.fantes.com
Cookware, bakeware, small appliances, cutlery.
(Romertopf, Schlemmertopf, Henckels, Chef's
Choice, Wüsthof, Krups, West Bend, Calphalon,
Kuhn Rikon, Atlas)

Gracious Home (2 locations in NYC)
1220 Third Avenue, New York, NY 10021
1-800-338-7800
1992 Broadway, New York, NY 10023
1-800-237-3404
www.gracioushome.com
Cookware, bakeware, small appliances, cutlery.
(KitchenAid, RevereWare, All-Clad, Le Creuset)

Kitchen, Etc. (14 stores, primarily in NH and
MA—1 in VA; call number below or see website
for locations)
1-800-232-4070
www.kitchenetc.com
Cookware, bakeware, small appliances, cutlery.
(Henckel, Farberware, Cuisinart, KitchenAid, Braun,
Krups, Revere Ware, Circulon, Rival, Oster)
Catalogue and mail order available

Korin Japanese Trading Corp.
57 Warren Avenue, New York, NY 10007
1-800-626-2172
www.korin.com
Wide range of Japanese restaurant products,
including kitchenware, equipment, and tableware.
Specializes in Japanese chef's knives and
professional utensils.

Tarzian Housewares
194 Seventh Avenue, Brooklyn, NY 11215
718-788-4213
Cookware, bakeware, kitchen gadgets, glassware,
small appliances, tableware. (All-Clad, Cuisinart,
Wüsthof, Oxo Good Grips, Emile Henry, Umbra)

The Pantry
P.O. Box 393, Titus Road, Washington Depot,
CT 06794
860-868-0258
Extensive selection of gadgets, utensils, accessories.
Also carries cookware, bakeware, cutting boards,
and bar accessories. (Zyliss, Saeco, Le Creuset, Oxo)

The Silo
44 Upland Road, New Milford, CT 06776
860-355-0300
www.thesilo.com
Cookware, bakeware, glassware,small appliances,
classes, cutlery. (Krups, Cuisinart, Wüsthof, Le
Creuset, Calphalon)

The Whip and Spoon
161 Commercial Street, Portland, ME 04101
1-800-937-9447
www.whipandspoon.com
Cookware, bakeware, food, wine, classes, gift
baskets, and more.
(Le Creuset, Calphalon, Bourgeat, Krups, Braun,
Cuisinart, KitchenAid, All-Clad)

SOUTHEAST

Campbell's Gourmet Cottage
127 North Sherrin Avenue, Louisville, KY 40207
502-893-6700
www.gourmetcottage.com
Extensive selection of high-quality cookware and
kitchen supplies. (All-Clad, Le Creuset, Nordic
Ware, Henckels, Wilton, Emile Henry, Rogar)

Complements to the Chef
374 Merrimon Avenue, Asheville, NC 28801
828-258-0558
1-800-895-CHEF
www.complementstothechef.com
Retailers of quality cookware and kitchen
accessories. (All-Clad, Henckels, Kuhn Rikon,
Calphalon, Romertopf, Endurance)

Metropolitan Kitchen
185 North Mill Court, Atlanta, GA 30328
1-888-892-9911
www.metrokitchen.com
Cookware, small appliances, cutlery, pot racks.
(All-Clad, Waring, Wüsthof, Dualit, Krups)

Rolling Pin Kitchen Emporium (35 stores in
Southeast and Midwest; call number below or see
website for store locations)
1-800-GADGETS
www.rollingpin.com
Cookware, bakeware, kitchen accessories, utensils,
gadgets, small appliances. (West Bend, Braun,
Capresso, Emile Henry, Chantal, All-Clad, Berndes,
Calphalon, Scanpan) Catalogue and mail order
available soon.

MIDWEST

The Cookery
140 North Main, Hudson, OH 44236
330-650-1665
Bakeware, cookware, utensils, gourmet food items.
(All-Clad, Le Creuset, Emile Henry, Mason Cash)

Kitchen Glamor (4 locations in MI; call number
below or see website for locations)
1-800-641-1252
www.kitchenglamor.com
Large selection of quality cooking and baking
equipment. (All-Clad, Cuisinart, Chantal, Le Creuset,
Scanpan, KitchenAid, Nordicware, Chicago Metallic,
Roscho) Catalogue and mail order available.

The Kitchen Port (3 locations in MI)
415 North Fifth Avenue, Ann Arbor, MI 48104
734-665-9188
800-832-7678
2621 Plymouth Road, Traver Village, MI 48105
734-930-1950
9864 East Grand River, Brighton, MI 48116
1-800-538-0333
Equipment, gadgets, and accessories for food
preparation, cooking, and dining. (All-Clad, Look, Le
Creuset, Calphalon, Capresso, Krups)

Kitchen Tools & Skills
26597 North Dixie Highway, Perrysburg, OH
43551
419-872-9090
1-800-288-6617
www.kitchentoolsandskills.com
Cookware, bakeware, gadgets, gourmet food items,
some small appliances. (Capresso, Calphalon, All-
Clad, Le Creuset, Kaiser, KitchenAid)

Kitchen Window
3001 Hennepin Ave., Minneapolis, MN 55408
612-824-4417
1-888-824-4417
www.kitchenwindow.com
Items for ethnic cooking, cookware, bakeware, small
appliances, kitchen tools, potracks, small appliances,
cutlery, gadgets. (All-Clad, Berndes, Chantal,
Calphalon, Wüsthof, Kaiser, Cuisinart, Krups, Bodum,
KitchenAid, Braun, Metallic)

Pickles, Peppers, Pots & Pans
101 West Madison St., Pontiac, IL 61764
1-888-845-4684
www.p4Online.com
Bakeware, cookware, small appliances, specialty
food, cutlery, cooking tools. (KitchenAid, All-Clad,
Kenwood, Leifheit, Waring, Calphalon, Le Creuset)

Rolling Pin Kitchen Emporium
404-264-1669
(see listing under Southeast)

Someone's In The Kitchen
2200 North Maple #554, Rapid City, SD 57701
605-341-5044
Bakeware, cookware, small appliances, gourmet
foods, cutlery, gadgets, utensils. (KitchenAid, All-
Clad, Henckels, Krups, Capresso, Calphalon,
Cuisinart)

SOUTHWEST

Capricorn Gourmet Cookware
100 Throckmorton Avenue, Mill Valley, CA 94941
415-388-1720
Cookware, bakeware, cutlery, cutting boards, wooden
kitchen equipment, kitchen gadgets, baskets. (All-Clad,
Calphalon, Le Creuset, Emile Henry, Henckels)

Chefstore
836 Traction Avenue, Los Angeles, CA 90013
213-617-2963
1-888-334-CHEF
www.chefstore.com
Professional tools, cookware, utensils, equipment.
(All-Clad, Kuhn-Rikon, Wüsthof Trident, Le Creuset,
KitchenAid)

Cooking
339 Divisadero Street, San Francisco, CA 94117
415-861-1854
Antique and used cookware.
(Brand selection varies—call to determine)

Dorothy McNett's Place
243 Sixth Street, Hollister, CA 95023
831-637-6444
www.happycookers.com
Gourmet cookware and kitchen shop. Quality
gadgets, cookware, utensils, cookbooks. (All-Clad,
Kuhn-Rikon, Master Chef)

Gift 'n Gourmet
55 Old Santa Fe Trail, Santa Fe, NM 87501
1-800-656-3234
Dinnerware, bakeware, glassware, flatware, cutlery,
cookware, gadgets. (Scanpan, Chantal, Berndes,
Henckels)

Homechef (8 stores in CA; call number below or
see website for locations)
415-927-3290
www.homechef.com
Cookware, bakeware, small appliances, cutlery.
(Emile Henry, BIA, Cuisinart, Waring, KitchenAid,
All-Clad, Wüsthof)

Kitchen Classics
4041 East Thomas Road, Phoenix, AZ 85018
1-888-954-3877
www.kitchen-classics.com
Small appliances, cookware, bakeware, cutting
equipment, kitchen gadgets and tools. (KitchenAid,
Cuisinart, Le Creuset, Nordic Ware, All-Clad, Kaiser,
John Boos)

Peppercorn
1235 Pearl St., Boulder, CO 80302
303-449-5847
1-800-447-6905
www.peppercorn.com
Cookware, appliances, dinnerware, kitchen
accessories, glassware. (Cuisinart, Calphalon,
Scanpan, Look, and many, many more)

Sur La Table (13 locations in Northwest and
Southwest; call number below or see website for
locations)
206-448-2244
1-800-243-0852
www.surlatable.com
Cookware, bakeware, exclusive line of copper
cookware, small appliances, gadgets, tabletop goods.
(Cuisinart, Waring, Wüsthof, Henckels, Global,
Krups, DeLonghi, Demeyere, All-Clad, Emile Henry,
KitchenAid) Catalogue and mail order available.

NORTHWEST

Kitchen Kaboodle (5 stores in the Portland area;
call number below or see website for locations)
1-800-366-0161
www.kitchenkaboodle.com
Small appliances, bakeware, cookware, cutlery,
kitchen basics, gadgets, decorative accessories.
(All-Clad, Cuisinart, Calphalon, Chantal)

Reed & Cross
160 Oakway Road, Eugene, OR 97401
514-484-1244
1-800-859-1244
www.reedcross.com
Kitchenware, dinnerware, cookware, appliances,
gourmet serving pieces, gadgets, cutlery. (Henckels,
All-Clad, Schlemmertopf, KitchenAid, Krups, Cuisinart)

Sur La Table
206-448-2244
1-800-243-2233 for mail order catalogue
www.surlatable.com
(see entry under Southwest)

NATIONAL CHAINSTORES

Bed, Bath and Beyond
(over 200 stores across the U.S.; call number below
or see website for store locations)
1-800-GoBeyond
www.bedbathandbeyond.com
Small appliances, cutlery, cookware, bakeware,
kitchen accessories. (All-Clad, Analon, Calphalon,
Cuisinart, KitchenAid, Pyrex, Proctor-Silex, Krups)

Crate and Barrel
(over 70 stores across the U.S.—none in Northwest.
Call number below or see website for locations)
1-800-967-6696
www.crateandbarrel.com
Kitchenware, cookware, bakeware, tableware,
textiles, glassware, utensils, barware (Cuisinart,
Krups, All-Clad, Berndes, Wüsthof, KitchenAid)
Catalogue and mail order available.

Dean & Deluca (stores in NY, CA, KS, NJ, NC and
Washington, DC; call number below or see website
for locations)
1-800-221-7714
www.deandeluca.com
Cookware, bakeware, cutlery, utensils, gadgets.
(Citroen, Paderno, Wüsthof, Global)

Dillards (over 300 stores in 29 states—none in
Northeast. Call number below or see website for
locations)
1-800-345-5273
www.dillards.com
Cookware, small small appliances, stemware,
flatware, china.
(Fiesta, Calphalon, KitchenAid, West Bend, Main
Ingredients)

Kitchen Collection (stores in 39 states; call number
below or see website for locations)
888-548-2651
www.kitchencollection.com
Cookware, bakeware, small appliances, and kitchen
utensils (Hamilton Beach, Proctor-Silex, KitchenAid,
Meyer Analon, Circulon and Bella Cuisine, Chef's
Best)

Linens 'n Things (over 215 stores in 38 states; call
number below or see website for locations)
1-800-LNT-8765
www.lnthings.com
Home textiles, housewares, small appliances,
decorative accessories, cookware, bakeware, cutlery
(Cuisinart, Rival, Calphalon, Krups, KitchenAid,
Wüsthof, Henckels)

Williams-Sonoma (192 stores in 29 states; call
number below or see website for locations)
1-800-541-2233
www.williams-sonoma.com
Bakeware, cookware, cutlery, small appliances,
utensils, gadgets.
(All-Clad, Braun, Calphalon, Cuisinart, Donvier,
Dulait, KitchenAid, Krups, Weber, Waring, Wüsthof)
Catalogue and mail order available.

MAIL ORDER

Chef's Catalogue
800-338-3232
Professional restaurant equipment for the home
chef. (Nordicware, Cuisinart, KitchenAid, Le
Creuset, Henckels)

Martha By Mail
800-950-7130
www.marthabymail.com
Essential kitchen tools and utensils, stoneware,
bakeware, molds, high-quality, hard-to-find
ingredients.

WEBSITES FOR ONLINE SHOPPING

www.cookingcompany.com
www.gourmetwarehouse.com
www.grandgourmet.com
www.kitchenshoppe.com
www.kitchenemporium.com
www.cheftools.com
www.procookware.com
www.cooking.com
www.tavolo.com
www.gourmetpalace.com
www.urbancook.com

index

publisher's acknowledgments

We would like to thank the following for contributing recipes to this book:

Page

15 Ken Hom: "Hong Kong-style broccoli and baby corn," © Ken Hom 2000;
19 Anne Willan: "summer squash salad," from *My Chateau Kitchen*, Clarkson Potter, © Anne Willan 2000
30 Charlie Trotter: "macadamia nut-crusted chicken breast with coconut-lemongrass emulsion," © Charlie Trotter 2000
35 Das Sreedharan: "coconut vegetable stew," © Das Sreedharan 2000
45 Jill Dupleix: "risotto with red wine and sausages," © Jill Dupleix 2000
60 Alain Ducasse: pumpkin and girolle soup and p62 "chicken stock," from *Ducasse Flavours of France*, Artisan, © Alain Ducasse 1998
61 Emi Kazuko: "ramen with pork and vegetables," © Emi Kazuko 2000
76 Paula Wolfert: "Tunisian couscous with greens, red peppers, and garlic," from *Mediterranean Cooking* (revised edition), HarperPerennial, © Paula Wolfert 1994
84 Raymond Blanc: "scallop and shiitake sir-fry," from *Blanc Vite*, Headline, © Raymond Blanc 1998
85 Madhur Jaffrey: "chicken in a red-pepper sauce," from *Madhur Jaffrey's Quick and Easy Cookery Course*, BBC Books, © Madhur Jaffrey 2000
90 Rose Gray and Ruth Rogers: "grilled squid with chilies," from *The River Cafe Cookbook*, Ebury, © Rose Gray and Ruth Rogers 1995
94 Wolfgang Puck: "barbecued seafood skewers with sun-dried tomato basil aïoli and grilled vegetable salad," © Wolfgang Puck 1993
95 Peter Gordon: "slightly smoky grilled quails with ginger, mirin, basil, and sesame," from *Cook at Home with Peter Gordon*, Hodder & Stoughton, © Peter Gordon 1999
100 Jamie Oliver: "pork and crackling," from *The Naked Chef*, Michael Joseph, © Jamie Oliver 1999
105 Claudia Roden: "chicken tagine with preserved lemons," from *Tamarind & Saffron*, Penguin Books, © Claudia Roden 1999
110 Alice Waters: "fresh shell bean gratin," from *Chez Panisse Vegetables*, HarperCollins, © Alice Waters 1996 Reprinted by permission of HarperCollins Publishers, Inc.
114 Marcella Hazan: "ricotta and mint tortelloni," from *Marcella Cucina*, HarperCollins, © Marcella Hazan 1997
118 Ursula Ferrigno and Eric Treuille: "Swedish dill bread," from *Bread*, Dorling Kindersley, © Ursula Ferrigno and Eric Treuille 1998

author's acknowledgments

I would like to thank Jacqui Small for asking me to write a book about one of my greatest passions. Thanks and appreciation to my editor, Stuart Cooper, for his good humor, guidance, and support throughout the project, and for his calmness in moments of crisis; and to my husband, Ed, for his generosity of spirit in allowing me to put the book before everything else.

I am deeply indebted to Jude Austin of the Bath branch of Kitchens, without whom the initial research would never have got off the ground; to Susan Campbell for kindly allowing me to use information from her own book *The Cook's Companion*; and to Michael Michaud and Robert Welch for their help and support. Thanks also to Roz Denny for contributing to the techniques pages; to Robin Rout for designing a beautiful book; to Mark Williams for the photography; to Josie Frater for locating the props; to Pippin Britz for preparing food for photography; and to Alexandra King for testing the recipes.

My appreciation and thanks also go to the chefs and food writers who contributed recipes—see "publisher's acknowledgments," right.

Finally, a special thank you to the numerous stores, manufacturers, and public relations companies who loaned items for photography.